*Tips for*

## *Public Speaking*

# DALE CARNEGIE

Selected from Carnegie's
Original 1920 YMCA Course Books

Edited by

Marie Carnegie Hill

E & E Publishing
Sausalito, California

E & E Publishing,
a Registered Trade Name of
THE E & E GROUP LLC
1001 Bridgeway, No. 227
Sausalito, California 94965
U.S.A.
EandEGroup@EandEGroup.com
www.EandEGroup.com/Publishing

Selections from *Public Speaking: The Standard Course of
the United Y.M.C.A. Schools*. Copyright 1920 & 1921 by The
International Committee of Young Men's Christian
Associations.

Publisher's Cataloging-In-Publication Data
(Prepared by The Donohue Group, Inc.)


Carnegie, Dale, 1888-1955.
  [Public speaking. Selections]
  Tips for public speaking : selected from Carnegie's original
1920 YMCA course books / edited by Marie Carnegie Hill.

    p. ; cm.

  ISBN-13: 978-0-9791606-3-9
  ISBN-10: 0-9791606-3-4

1. Public speaking.  2. Business presentations.  I. Hill, Marie
Carnegie.  II. Title.  III. Title: Public speaking. Selections

PN4121 .C25 2007
808.5/1


Printed in U.S.A.

# Contents

# Editor's Note

Dale Carnegie's *Tips for Public Speaking* is an updated edition of Carnegie's seminal work, the four course books in public speaking published by the YMCA in 1920. These course books are unduplicated by later works.

Here is the authentic Dale Carnegie, both folksy and erudite, teaching us not only Courage and Self-Confidence, but the secrets of Opening and Closing an Address; Preparing the Speech; giving the Convincing Speech, the Popular Speech, the Humorous Speech, the Impressive Speech, and much more.

Carnegie shows that public speaking is the ideal vehicle for people in all walks of life to gain the self-confidence that brings success in all their endeavors.

While Carnegie cites public figures well-known in the 1920s, the principles are equally vital and valid today.

For easy reference, the *Tips* have been numbered consecutively throughout the book.

— Marie Carnegie Hill

# *From the Author*

The following is my own story, which I hope may serve as a guidepost to the thoughtful student:

*The first thirty years of my life I was mentally asleep. I utilized only about ten percent of my mental powers and wondered why I did not get ahead.*

Finally, I was shocked into finding myself. A new department was being formed in our company. I was more familiar than anyone else with the work it would have to perform. Several other men openly coveted the position of manager of this new department.

I was called before a session of the board of directors to express my ideas regarding its administration. I approached that conclave with trembling. The very presence of these superior officers confused me, and I was unable to answer their questions intelligently. Finally one of them turned to the chairman and inquired, "Does this man know what he is talk about?" I did. But only a mind reader could have detected the fact. When I left that room, I knew that my chance for the coveted position had vanished into thin air.

That failure was the best thing that ever happened to me. When I got home that night, I threw my collar and tie on the bed, not caring where they fell, lit my pipe and sat down in the darkness to think things through. I sat there for hours asking myself questions. Why was I not able to associate with certain men at the office? Why had they never asked me to their homes? What differentiated me from the men who forged ahead socially and in business? There was a big gulf between us, I knew.

That night I resolved to cultivate assiduously the qualities that I lacked and that men of presence and command possessed. I was sure that I should never possess a strong personality, but I had an abiding faith—which the years have justified—that I could treble over and over again the infinitesimal amount I then possessed. *Every man has in him dormant powers of which he never dreams.*

I read several books on psychology and personality. I discussed the subject with other people. I studied the magnetic men I met.

*I made this valuable discovery regarding them: they were buoyant, enthusiastic, and optimistic.*

I also found that these moods were contagious. One sweltering July afternoon, I passed a yard where a number of children clad in bathing suits were hilariously turning the hose upon one another. I stopped and was soon laughing and vicariously enjoying the sport as much as they.

Delight and hope are always attractive and magnetic; gloom and despair, never. I immediately instituted a program to cultivate a sort of I-am-glad-to-be-alive feeling.

One day I met a friend on the street, and he said enthusiastically, "Isn't this a glorious day?"

I hadn't taken time to think whether it was or not, but I agreed to his statement in a perfunctory way.

He grabbed my arm. "See here," he objected, "don't think you are going to get away with it in that fashion. Take a little time to live. Get out of your rut. Drink in the spirit of the day. Look at that sky—and those clouds. It is a sight to stir your soul."

When I walked down the street five minutes later, my steps were lighter, and I caught myself unconsciously humming a tune.

After that incident, I began to take time to feel the sunlight and the west wind striking my face. I took time to admire sunsets and dawns.

*I discovered that my attitude during the first half hour after I awoke, usually colored the rest of the day; so I forced myself to be cheerful for the first thirty minutes.* I compelled myself to whistle and hum and smile and think cheerful thoughts, no matter what the day held for me. I found that if I did that for the first half hour, the rest of the day my voice was more cheerful and there was more sunlight in my expression.

One glad day, Edward James Cattell, one of the best-known after-dinner speakers in this country, spoke in our town. During the course of his address, *he said that he had not, in the past ten years, passed anyone on the street who seemed to be less fortunate than he, without touching his hand to his hat and silently thanking the Creator for His kindness to Mr. Cattell.* He has practiced this for years. It has made him more sympathetic, happier, and more contented with his lot.

I have read somewhere that the poet Longfellow told Mary Anderson, the actress, that she could develop voice charm by reading aloud each day a joyous lyric poem. This develops the bright tones of the voice, and bright tones are always the magnetic tones.

Emerson said, "When a man lives with God, his voice shall be as sweet as the murmur of the brook and the rustle of the corn."

The spirit of contentment and optimism and courage that is developed in these divers ways, radiates through your speaking. It helps you to converse and to make friends.

A little observation has shown me that undue haste is a sign of littleness—an indication that events are too much for one. *Big men, I observed, have poise. They are masters of the situa-*

*tion; no matter how hard the stress of circum-
stances becomes, they maintain an inner control of
themselves.*

This is an ideal condition which I resolved
to attain. I didn't just idly wish that I might have
poise. I wanted it earnestly—and was willing to pay
the price to get it. A dozen times a day I would stop,
relax for a moment, breathe deeply and picture to
myself the self-controlled individual I would surely
become. I soon began to realize in my own life this
ideal condition which I constantly held before me
and strove to attain.

I have read many times a little book by
James Allen entitled "As a Man Thinketh," and
regard it as one of the most illuminating treatises in
the English language. It pointed out more clearly to
me than anything else had ever done that "self
control is strength; right thought is mastery." It
also taught me that I, being master of my thought,
was therefore the maker and shaper of my condition and destiny. I soon began to realize in my own
life the ideal condition which I constantly held
before me and strove to attain.

We are speaking now of poise and self-
control, and I know of nothing else that will impart
these qualities so surely as the feeling and faith of
religion.

William Cullen Bryant was riding horseback

in New England one evening when he saw a water fowl winging its way through "the desert and illimitable air." That trivial incident inspired Bryant to write one of his best known poems—"To a Waterfowl." I often repeat its closing verse:

"He who, from zone to zone,
Guides through the boundless sky thy certain flight,
In the long way that I must tread alone,
Will lead my steps aright."

A spirit of inner peace and serenity descends upon a man when he comes to feel that the Creator who guides the waterfowl in his flight and keeps the stars singing in their orbits, will also guide his steps aright.

Whenever I am worried and harassed, I open my Bible before retiring for the night and read the 91st Psalm. Countless thousands of soldiers used to read that Psalm in France before the zero hour. It instills in a man an abiding courage, and faith, and trust to read such promises as these:
"A thousand shall fall at thy side,
And ten thousand at thy right hand;
But it shall not come nigh thee...
For he will give his angels charge over thee.
To keep thee in all they ways.
They shall bear thee up in their hands,
Lest thou dash thy foot against a stone."

I said at the very outset of my tale, that I have studied the magnetic men I met. These men were, I found, self-confident. They radiated a sure faith in their own ability to do things and boundless courage to try and carry through.

Of such stuff is magnetism made. Fear and doubts always repel. Courage and confidence attract.

I had never heard of a public speaking course at that time, but I persuaded half a dozen of my friends to form a debating club. We used to meet at one another's houses, make extemporaneous speeches, and debate on all manner of questions. I was frankly surprised at the rapidity with which this practice gave all of us self-confidence; it gave us courage not only to stand up and address an audience but it gave us confidence in all our daily activities.

This debating and public speaking club gave me a hunger for more knowledge. One day while browsing through some books, I chanced upon a poem which has exercised a decisive influence in my life—a stirring poem by Henley—"Invictus." Its author was an invalid most of his life; he rarely knew the luxury of being free from the pain of a surgeon's knife; but in spite of his physical affliction, he wrote what Dr. Frank Crane told me was regarded as, *"The finest spiritual declaration in our language."*

    I have read that this was also Roosevelt's favorite poem. I was so impressed with this poem that I memorized it and delivered it at one of the meetings of our debating society. I shall set it down here, hoping that it may quicken and strengthen others as it served and stimulated me. I hope that you will memorize this poem and make it your creed:

Out of the night that covers me,
    Black as the pit from pole to pole,
I thank whatever gods may be
    For my unconquerable soul.

In the fell clutch of circumstance
    I have not winced nor cried aloud;
Under the bludgeonings of change
    My head is bloody, but unbowed.
Beyond this place of wrath and tears
    Looms but the Horror of the shade,
And yet the menace of the years
    Finds and shall find me unafraid.

It matters not how strait the gate,
    How charged with punishments the scroll,
I am the master of my fate:
    I am the captain of my soul.
              — William Ernest Henley

Half of the time I did not feel well—headaches and that sort of thing. No man is going to generate much power of any kind when his bodily engine is missing fire on half of its cylinders.

*Magnetism is founded on vivacity, not sluggishness.*

I started to make myself "a better animal"; my home was a mile from the office, and I arose early enough so that I could walk and breathe deeply each morning. I slept longer, drank twice as much water as I had formerly done, ate about half as much, and paid more respect to all the laws of hygienic living. The results were a little slow at first, but I soon had the blood leaping through my arteries, and I felt and reflected the exuberance of perfect health. I generated greater staying powers and cast off the languid feeling that had so often sapped my vitality.

All these things had made a marked difference in my conversation and my ability to meet and interest people; but I had not yet discovered the biggest factor in magnetism. It was revealed to me one night by the most noted lecturer in our state. I had heard him many times and had made a careful study of the manner in which he obtained his effects. I was particularly delighted and moved by one of his addresses, and I wrote him to express my appreciation. This little act of kindness on my part resulted in what was one of the turning points of my life; for he invited me to come to see him.

My story interested him, and he talked freely out of his long experience.

*"Magnetism,"* he said, *"is reserve power."*

He talked to me for hours about the eminent people he had known.

"Mansfield," he reminisced, "was a magnetic actor because of his reserve power and versatility; he could paint, and dance, and direct the orchestra as well as act. And Kipling told me when I was in London that he often wrote his short stories four times as long as they finally appeared in the magazines. The things that he wrote and then eliminated, colored what he left in. The things that he knew and didn't say, put reserve power into what he did express.

"Many years ago Ida M. Tarbell, the noted author, was assigned to write an article on "The Atlantic Cable" for *McClure's Magazine.* She interviewed the general manager for the cable, and acquired all the information necessary to write the article. But she did not stop with the necessary information: she studied a display of cables in the British Museum and visited plants that manufactured cables. She never used this additional information, but the possession of it gave her reserve power and put magnetism into her writing."

This white-haired lecturer told me how he

had discovered this principle in his own speaking. When he told his audience all he knew about a subject, it usually failed to impress them: when he spoke out of a vast untouched reservoir of knowledge, his words were charged with dynamic force.

In the subdued light of his library that night, that venerable speaker imparted an impulse to me which has doubled my capacity for enjoyment. *He introduced to me a new world: a world where I commanded kings, and knaves, and heroes to stand and deliver to me accounts of their adventures and lives. I was crowned emperor in the delightful dominion of books.*

He made plain to me that I didn't have enough mental reserve power stored away to make a magnetic speaker. I went home that night with a new vision, a high intent—and a book under my arm.

I learned to utilize the spare moments that I had been wasting.

Richard Washburn Child told me that he often wrote stories in taxicabs. Every line of his novel "The Blue Wall" was written in Pullman cars. Jack London used to carry a book with him when he went to the corner grocery. If he had to wait before he could give his order, he utilized these otherwise wasted moments in reading. *It is not so much a lack of time, as a lack of will power to utilize odd minutes, that prevents the average man from accomplishing more.*

I also found out that to get the desired results I had to have system and order in my reading. It is easy to do the things that have become habitual, so I made reading on Monday, Tuesday, and Friday nights a habit. These were my nights for mental growth, and nothing was allowed to interfere with that schedule. When I resolved to read just as I happened to have the time, my good intentions proved as fragile as Dresden china.

I am often asked by business men to recommend a course of reading. This is difficult, for what interests one man will bore another. I would suggest that each man consult the librarian in his home city. I have often recommended the Chautauqua Course of Reading conducted by the Chautauqua Institute, Chautauqua, New York. Many young men have thanked me for calling such books as these to their attention: "The Secret of Achievement," by Orison Swett Marden; "Great Books as Life Teachers," by Newell Dwight Hillis.

This lecturer loaned me, among other books, Ridpath's History of the World. I shall never forget the avidity with which I read for the first time, the story of the human race: its loves and hates, its sorrows and wars, its adventures and discoveries. I used to arise an hour earlier than necessary each morning, so that I might continue the story.

*My penchant for reading enriched my life in a way that only those who love books can understand. It doubled my capacity for enjoyment. It made me an inhabitant of every clime and heir of all the ages.* Professor Agassiz was my guide along the Silurian beach when the world was young. I discovered with Livingstone the famous Victoria Falls of the Zambesi. I lived with Thoreau at Walden Pond.

I was present at every dramatic episode of history: I saw Troy fall; I stood with Leonidas at Thermopylae; with Charles Martel I hammered back the Saracens at Tours; I fought with Cromwell at Marston Moor; I saw the Magna Charta wrested from King John; I saw by the light of a stormy sunset, a cart issuing from the gate of the Conciergerie, and I saw in it, sheathed in a red smock, Charlotte Corday riding to the guillotine.

I walked with all the great men from Plutarch's heroes to Lincoln. I made the acquaintance of all the inventors from Gutenberg to Edison. All the poets from Homer to Kipling sang for me. All the essayists from Bacon to Emerson and all the philosophers from Socrates to Spencer counseled me and talked to me of Life.

I now understand the cause of the difference that one usually feels between the educated and the unread man: one has a vast store of reserve power;

the other's knowledge and experiences have been limited to his own narrow sphere and what he has heard from a few companions.

And what a difference all of this made in my bearing, personality, and address!

I had in a few years changed even the expression of my face and the light that shone from my eyes!

Men who occupied positions above me often came and sat on the edge of my desk to discuss current events and to ask my advice about their problems. I was invited out socially oftener than I could accept. My conversation seemed to interest people and to carry weight—things it had never done before.

I was scheduled for an address at the annual dinner of the employees of our company. When I stood up to speak that evening, I felt sure of myself, for I had carefully prepared my address and had repeated it a score of times to my dog. I had also been practicing speaking on my feet in a debating society, and I felt that I knew more about the art of public speaking than any of my auditors did; and the realization of that gave me confidence.

I shall never forget the feeling of infinite satisfaction that flooded over me as I stood there realizing that I was commanding the attention and shaping the thoughts, and beliefs, and actions of my auditors. There are few happier moments in a man's life than those in which he exercises power over an audience. It is a delight that nothing else can give.

My thirty-minute address was followed by long and enthusiastic applause. When I went home that night, I felt that I had found myself—that I was coming into my own.

What a difference between this night and my pitiful attempt of a few years previous to answer the questions of a board of directors!

That autumn the general manager of our company was shot while hunting deer in Maine. I was given his position.

I spoke in public often after that. Two years later I addressed the Chamber of Commerce of a large eastern city. A fortnight later I received a telegram from a man who had sat in that audience, asking me to meet him at the Astor Hotel in New York.

After several interviews I became general manager and member of a firm manufacturing a line of hardware and automobile specialties. The results in a financial way have surpassed my most sanguine expectations.

For the past five years I have had leisure to devote to the hobby of my life—public speaking. In the last few years I have addressed business organizations and groups of young business men in every state in our Union. I am trying to do for others what this venerable white-haired lecturer did for me many years ago: I am trying to inspire young men to cultivate themselves. In this way I am trying to repay the great debt that I owe to my counselor.

Gratifying as my increased remuneration has been, it never has been and never can be the chief harvest that I have garnered from the seeds of personal development. My most satisfying return has been this: an inner realization of my own progress and the uncovering and fruition of my hidden powers. For, after all, the true test of a man's success is, not what he has, but what he is.

— Dale Carnegie

One

# *Courage*

## 1. Courage

"With morale, confidence and spirit, fifty men can beat two hundred."—*Leadership and Military Training.*

—Lieut. Col. Andrews, U.S.A.

*"Success is the child of audacity."*

—Beaconsfield

"A great deal of talent is lost to the world for the want of a little courage. Every day sends to their graves a number of obscure men who have only remained in obscurity because their timidity prevented them from making the first effort, and who, if they could only have been induced to begin, would in all probability have gone great lengths in the career of fame...."         —Sydney Smith

## 2. Learn to Use Your Powers

No man knows what he can do until he has tried. No man can realize the powers which have been given him until he learns to use them. But we do know, thanks to that great psychologist, Professor James, that the average man develops only ten percent of his mental powers. Imagine a ten-cylinder motor car traveling on but one cylinder, and you have a picture of—perhaps yourself.

## 3. Public Speaking in Business

Ninety percent of the classes in public speaking are composed of businessmen—salesmen, advertisers, brokers, builders, and artisans. Many of these men have no present intention of using this asset before large audiences; but they are enthusiastic students. Listen to these statements:

*"Every session was worth a thousand dollars to me. My sales doubled the first year."*

*"I have never made a public speech since I took the course, but I notice that I now get fifty percent more replies to my letters. That is what it did for me."*

*"I used to enter the room of our president like a humble peasant asking a boon from the king. Now I meet him as an equal, and I usually get what I go after."*

## 4. Speaking in the Professions

Who are the most influential preachers in your local churches? What lawyers win the most cases in your courts? What public officials in your county wield the greatest power in local politics? They are the men who are the most effective speakers. It was of these that Shakespeare was thinking when he said, "Mend your voice lest it mar your fortune."

~ ~ ~

The old Roman who said that "poets are born" was good enough to add "but orators are made." This should forever silence the pessimist who moans that he was not blessed with the gift of oratory.

## 5. Public Speaking in Social Life

Whether you appear as an after-dinner speaker, or as a quiet conversationalist, the test of your success is the same. For public speaking is little more than enlarged conversation. And the rules which point the way to success on a platform are the same as those which compel attention in private conversation. A speech is only a high-grade, well-prepared conversation.

## 6. Self-Confidence is the Supreme Goal

The first thing that you must acquire in Public Speaking is self-confidence. It is the first factor in the success of any undertaking.

There is one certain way to acquire confidence. Do the thing you fear to do and you conquer fear. Make this your slogan: "I will do the thing that I know I ought to do, but fear to do."

I gladly and boldly assure you that you can conquer your fear if you will only despair not, but practice often.

*You are going to conquer fear.*

## 7. The Vision and the Victory

The mere reading of books on public speaking—that alone will never make you a confident speaker any more than perusing a treatise on tennis playing or swimming will make you proficient in those sports without getting out your racquet or bathing suit, and getting busy on the tennis court or in the swimming pool.

## 8. Practice

Don't pass up a turn to speak when it comes. Speak on something that you are familiar with, something concerning your business or profession. Speak every time the occasion permits.

No effort will be lost. Each time, regardless of whether you realize it or not, you will be nearing your ultimate goal of self-confidence before an audience.

## 9. Trust Yourself

You have talked all your life. Now don't imagine that public speaking is something strange and difficult and mysterious. Don't think you have to "throw a fit" or do some mental gymnastics when you make a public address.

When you start speaking, *trust yourself*. You are never afraid that your stomach won't digest a beefsteak, or that your lungs will cease to breathe, or your heart to beat. And if you are prepared, you can trust your brain to feed you thoughts and words before an audience.

## 10. If You Feel Nervous

Before speaking in public, breathe deeply through your nostrils. Deep breathing is a remarkable help. It will buoy you up and give you courage.

If you still feel nervous, grasp some solid object: a bunch of keys, a coin, or the back of a chair. You will find that if you can grasp a solid object when you are a bit excited, it brings you down to terra firma and helps you to get hold of yourself.

## 11. Know Your Subject

Know a great deal more about your subject than you have time to tell in your speech: your reserve power will aid your confidence.

## 12. *Think Victory*

Think victory. See yourself in your imagination speaking to an audience in the self-confident, victorious manner that you aspire to possess. Have faith. The Master Speaker of all time taught us that faith, even as a grain of mustard seed, will remove mountains.

## 13. *Correct Breathing*

The Sanskrit writers said thousands of years ago in India: "He who only half breathes, half lives." Physicians estimate that the average man could lengthen his life from three to ten years by practicing deep breathing five minutes daily as he walks along the street.

Learn to breathe in this way: begin to breathe at the waist line and fill your lungs as one fills a glass from the bottom up. Do not raise your shoulders and try to enlarge your lungs at the top. The apex of the lungs is encased in a bony box made by the ribs and backbone; your lungs have little chance to expand at the top. Learn to breathe from the waist.

Breathe in deeply through the nostrils. Hold the breath for five seconds; then exhale slowly, through the mouth, with a steady and even hissing sound. Repeat this exercise before an open window ten minutes each morning; it will tone you up for the day.

Two

# *Enthusiasm*

## 14. Enthusiasm

*"Be intensely in earnest....Enthusiasm invites enthusiasm."* — Russell H. Conwell, author of "Acres of Diamonds"

*"Genius is intensity. The man who gets anything worth having is the man who goes after his object as a bulldog goes after a cat—with every fiber in him tense with eagerness and determination."* — W.C. Holman, formerly Sales Manager, National Cash Register Co.

*"Every great and commanding movement in the annals of history is the triumph of enthusiasm."* — Emerson

*"Enthusiasm doubles the power to think and do. It helps its possessor to dominate any situation. The man or woman of enthusiastic trend always exercises a magnetic influence over those with whom he or she comes in contact....Enthusiasm means dollars in your pockets as well as a ruddier glow on your cheeks."*

— H. Addington Bruce

## 15. Value of Positive Language

The almost universal trouble with beginning speakers is not that they are too positive, but that they vitiate their talks with "weasel" phrases, as Theodore Roosevelt called them, such as "It seems to me," "I think," "perhaps it may be correct." Timid, apologetic tones and phrases convince no one and get their author rated only as a weakling.

## 16. Choice of Live Topics

Talk about things that you like. The big things that appeal to you are pretty likely to interest other people also.

But many men have confessed to me that there was nothing in which they were especially interested and they didn't know what to speak about! Man alive! If this is true, then you are only half awake! Then you are only half living!

Get a copy of *USA Today*, or *Time Magazine*, or *National Geographic* and knock off for a couple of hours this evening and find out what mankind is thinking about and struggling for. Study these stories of the day again and again until you are interested. If you delve deeply enough into any subject, you will find yourself becoming interested in it.

Now try this fresh interest of yours on your friends, in conversation and in a talk in public. You can put it across in a fashion that will surpass your most sanguine expectations.

## 17. Ways That Convince

A sales manager instructed his salesmen to develop enthusiasm and conviction in the following manner:

"You get off around a corner somewhere where you can be alone, and sell *yourself* a line of the article we make. Think over its value; realize it; burn it into your mind. Enumerate its good qualities one after the other; get a realizing sense of each one. Consider what our product will do for a business man, the money it will make for him, the saving it will effect. Sweep out of your mind, like so many cobwebs, any apologetic feeling regarding it. You are not trying to trick or cajole him into doing something that he can't afford to do. You are helping him to increase his profits. You are doing him as great a favor as he does you.

"Say these things over to yourself. Think them in your heart, realize them—they're all true."

—"Ginger Talks," by W. C. Holman.

Speakers have often used similar tactics to develop enthusiasm regarding their subjects. One student at the New York City Chapter of the American Institute of Banking essayed to talk about Thrift, but at first his talks failed, because he lacked vitality. Then he started to "sell" himself thoroughly on the idea. He burned into his mind these facts, shown by the Probate Court records in New York: More than 85.3 percent of the people leave nothing at death; only 3.3 percent leave over $10,000. He thought over the appalling fact that more than 50 percent of men at sixty-five years of age are dependent upon children, relatives, or charity for support. He told himself that he was not asking people to do something that they could not afford to do, but that he was preparing them to have meat and bread and clothes in their old age. He repeated this to himself until he made himself feel so keenly the necessity for Thrift that his earnestness convinced others.

His talks impressed the officials of another bank, and he was given a place in their organization at an increased salary.

## 18. Daily Practice in Speaking

After you have dealt with crowds a while you will discover that there is nothing people need so much as a leader—someone to voice what they have believed and felt all the time, but did not have the confidence to say.

Tonight take a stroll by yourself and frame up a little "speech" on a subject that you have been wanting for months to get off your chest, perhaps relating to a change you would like to be made in some business organization, some club or lodge.

Make the "speech" short and direct. Have it positive, snappy.

Try it over to yourself several times during the evening. Imagine you are saying it to one of the men or the audience you are going to try it on.

Tomorrow, when you meet one of these individuals, swing the conversation around to your subject, and fire it off at him. Try it, if possible, on a dozen different ones.

Your interest in the matter is bound to attract attention. If you have not been in the habit of doing this sort of thing, people will begin remarking, "What has come over George?"

If you deliver this same "speech" before the organization for whom it is intended, it will swing the spotlight on to you. It will get you noticed.

*A few public addresses in any organization usually mean that the speaker will be appointed to committees and elected to positions of honor.*

## 19. Speech Building

When preparing a talk, be clear in your own mind as to what you want to do—i.e., to give information, to amuse, to convince, to get action—and select your material and arrange it with your purpose in mind. Make sure you have the right words to give your meaning and accomplish your purpose. Look up meaning and pronunciation of words, if in doubt. Practice and get command of your material.

## 20. Power of the Voice

*"The average man who attempts to speak in public can't be heard twenty feet away."* — George W. Wickersham, former U.S. Attorney General

The student invariably insists in using normal conversational tones on the platform. When he speaks with sufficient vitality to be effective, he will think that he is fairly shouting and that people will laugh at him. Conversational tones are exactly the effect desired, but they must be enlarged.

The public speaking voice bears about the same relation to the private speaking voice that the small print in a newspaper bears to the headlines. The small type in the columns is sufficient when the sheet is held eighteen inches from the eyes. Nothing but bold headlines, however, can be read one hundred feet distant.

The type in the headlines is similar to the type in the reading matter—except it is enlarged.

In quite the same manner, the conversational speaking voice must be made bigger when addressing an audience.

*Mere loudness that makes itself heard is not sufficient. A speech must have more than vocal force: it must radiate vitality, earnestness, and spirit. Those are the qualities that command attention and convince.*

## 21. Enthusiasm & Power

When you become intensely interested in your talk, you will forget your fears, you will gain self-confidence, and your enthusiasm will carry the crowd with you.

If you speak with a deep sincerity and whole-heartedness, your hearers will be imbued with your spirit.

The positive man radiates conviction and power. If you are timid and apologetic and lacking in confidence, force yourself to *speak out* like a man with red blood leaping through his arteries, and you will see your little world veer around and take a different tack towards you.

## 22. The Will to Conquer

You can, right now, loosen up, let yourself go, and speak with earnest, convincing tones that will impress a large audience. There is no question about it, if you only summon up your power of self-direction and command yourself.

No one can make a speaker of you except yourself. We instructor-physicians can prescribe the medicine, but no one under the Milky Way can take it for you. It is strictly up to you.

The Apostle Paul said, "every man must work out his own salvation." You will have to work out your salvation as a speaker. The sooner you realize it, the sooner you summon up your will power and force yourself to speak out courageously like a man, the sooner will you realize your ambitions.

# Three

## *Memory*

## 23. Memory

*"To be intimate with your audience is half the battle, and nothing so restricts and impedes that intimacy as the presence of a scrap of paper."*
— Thomas W. Higginson

*"The speeches (in the House of Commons) that were really listened to, that were enjoyed, that carried the force of conviction, were the speeches that were spoken without reference to notes."* — Charles Seymour

*"When I intend to speak on anything that seems to me important I consider what it is that I wish to impress upon my audience. I do not write my facts or my arguments, but make notes on two or three or four slips of note paper, giving the line of argument and the facts as they occur to my mind, and I leave the words to come at call while I am speaking. There are occasionally short passages which for accuracy, I may write down; as sometimes, also—almost invariably—the concluding words or sentences may be written."*
— John Bright

Reading an address from a manuscript only bores an audience. If you memorize your address word for word, your delivery will be cold and formal, and your audience will not warm up to you.

## 24. Everyday Language vs. Polished Diction

If the language that you use in conversation isn't fit for the platform, then there is something wrong with your everyday grammar and choice of words, and your language should have thoughtful attention immediately. You had better give your English an overhauling.

## 25. A Large Dictionary

If you don't already possess a large dictionary, you should invest in one immediately.

## 26. Business English

Three-fourths of the men who enroll for this course in Public Speaking could with much profit study also a course in Business English.

## 27. Association of Ideas

You will find that you can remember ideas very easily if you tie them together like the huskies in an arctic dog team.

You can memorize the outline of an address with delightful swiftness by using that little trick.

*a. Memorize a key sentence formed from the main words in your outline.*

Not long ago, I was hastily called upon for a Sunday address. I had only five minutes' advance notice and I decided to mention: first, the impracticability of a religion that does not touch everyday life; second, the need for a religion that deals with the economics of modern life; and I hastily chose illustrations from the activities of James J. Hill, Henry Ford, and The Guaranty Trust Co., New York.

I was able to memorize this outline instantly by tying these five ideas together in this nonsensical sentence: "An impractical and economical hill made Ford guarantee his cars."

To be sure the sentence is nonsensical. But the more nonsensical and ridiculous it is, the more readily you can recall it when facing an audience.

*b. Memorize a key word made out of the initial letters of your main points.*

Many ministers remember their outlines by fashioning a word from the initial letters of the words representing their main points. To illustrate: if you desired to speak about four elements of delivery, Rate of Speaking, Emphasis, Pause, and Pitch, you could work the four initial letters into the word *PREP*.


## 28. Illustrations as Aids to Memory

Illustrations are concrete things—usually things we can see. You are able, aren't you, to remember the illustrations in a talk infinitely better than to remember the abstract thoughts?

Here are two paragraphs that will enable you to test this thing out now for yourself. One deals largely with general statements; the other with concrete illustrations. Which is the easier to remember?

1. Our great inventors often secured their ideas from the most common sources. They observed the things that countless generations of men had seen, but the inventors observed with imagination. They saw beyond the mere incident, and their intellects utilized the principles underlying these homely happenings to create tools for mankind.

2. A cat thrusting her claws between the slats in a chicken coop and pulling off feathers from the inmates, gave Eli Whitney the idea for the cotton gin. Whitney's acute mind saw instead of the chicken crate, a box of cotton. In his imagination the wooden slats became steel wires. He beheld instead of the cat's claws, steel hooks reaching between the wires and pulling cotton from the seeds in the box, just as the cat had pulled feathers between the slats.

## 29. Mark Twain's Secret for Memorizing a Speech

Mark Twain, in an article which he wrote for *Harper's Magazine*, lifted the embargo on his secret for memorizing the outline of an address. I have tested the recipe which he gives here, and, believe me, it works.

"Dates are hard to remember because they consist of figures: figures are monotonously un-striking in appearance, and they don't take hold; they form no pictures, and so they give the eye no chance to take hold. Pictures make dates stick. They can make nearly anything stick—particularly if you make the picture yourself. Indeed, that is the great point—make the picture yourself. I know about this from experience. Thirty years ago I was delivering a memorized lecture every night, and every night I had to help myself with a page of notes to keep from getting myself mixed. The notes consisted of beginnings of sentences, and were eleven in number, and they ran something like this:

In that region the weather—

At that time it was a custom—

But in California one never heard—

"Eleven of them. They initialed the brief of the lecture and protected me against skipping. But they all looked about alike on the page; they formed no picture; I had them by heart, but I could never with certainty remember the order of their succession; therefore I always had to keep those notes by me and look at them every little while. Once I mislaid them; you will not be able to imagine the terrors of that evening. I now saw that I must invent some other protection. So I got ten of the initial letters by heart in their proper order—I, A, B, and so on—and I went on the platform the next night with these marked in ink on my ten finger-nails. But it didn't answer. I kept track of the fingers for awhile; then I lost it, and after that I was never quite sure which finger I had used last. I couldn't lick off a letter after using it, for while that would have made success certain, it would also have provoked too much curiosity. There was curiosity enough without that. To the audience I seemed more interested in my finger nails than I was in my subject; one or two persons asked afterward what was the matter with my hands.

"It was then that the idea of pictures occurred to me; then my troubles passed away. In two minutes I made six pictures with my pen, and they did the work of the eleven catch-sentences and did it perfectly. I threw the pictures away as soon as they were made, for I was sure I could shut my eyes and see them any time. That was a quarter of a century ago; the lecture vanished out of my head more than twenty years ago, but I could rewrite it from the pictures—for they remain."

## 30. My Application of Mark Twain's Method for Memorizing a Speech

I am going to set down here rather minute directions showing how a number of men have used Mark Twain's method of memorizing not only the points of an address, but also their order.

I know from experience that many readers will "pooh-pooh" this plan as being asinine, and more difficult than the old-fashioned hammer-and-tongs method of fixing a thing in mind by the sheer force of repetition.

The experience of many men, however, is to the contrary.

By this method and within fifteen minutes, I have taught the most skeptical men to repeat in the order named fifteen or twenty objects that had been called to them just once.

I also know that many men find this picture plan immensely practical in remembering speech outlines.

You, of course, will accept or reject it according to the dictates of your own good judgment.

I have done it crudely, I admit, but this is the manner in which I employ Mark Twain's memory system:

I turn all of my main ideas into pictures, also the order of their succession. I then combine the two pictures. Suppose that the second thing I wanted to discuss in my outline was *submarines*: I would picture in my mind's eye a submarine in a *zoo*—*zoo* sounds like *two*, and it is the picture that I use to remember what is coming *second*.

Here is a list of pictures that I have made to represent all the numbers from 1 to 20.

1. *bum* or a man with a *bun on*, an intoxicated man

2. *zoo*: see the animals walking about behind iron bars

3. *tree*

4. *fort*

5. a bee *hive*

6. a *sick* person

7. streets of gold in *Heaven*

8. *gate*

9. *wine* or *kine* (cattle)

10. a writing *pen* or a *den* of wild animals

11. a football team (*eleven* players)

12. a *shelf*

13. a man with something *hurting* him

14. a couple *courting*

15. a man *lifting* something

16. a man *licking* or thrashing another

17. a woman kneading dough that has been *leavened*

18. a person *waiting*

19. a woman *pining*

20. *ten at tea* (ten old women drinking tea)

Now let me show you how I applied this system to memorizing a brief for a speech recently. I desired to mention the following points in the order indicated:

First: Strikes
Second: Compulsory Industrial Arbitration
Third: Wages
Fourth: High Cost of Living
Fifth: Profit Sharing
Sixth: Loyalty

Seventh: Welfare Work

I formed in my mind's eye a rough sketch something like that on the following page: you will observe that the picture of a *Strike* (the first idea in our speech) is connected with a *bum* (the picture for the number, *one*).

We have there a picture of some capitalists and workmen trying to *Arbitrate* (our second idea) in a *zoo* (our picture for number *two*).

There is a sketch of a quarter of beef with a price tag of "$5 a lb." on it to represent the *High Cost of Living* (our fourth idea) and you notice that the beef in hung on the side of a *fort* (our picture for the number, *four*).

There is a capitalist giving a bag of money, *Sharing* his *Profits*, with a laborer (our fifth idea) and the capitalist is sitting on a *bee hive* (our picture code for the number, *five.*)

You can make your own picture for the last two ideas. Make a rough sketch that will represent *Loyalty* and connect it with a picture of *sickness* (the picture for number *six*). In like manner, draw a picture that will connect *Welfare Work* with the streets of gold in *Heaven* (for the number *seven*).

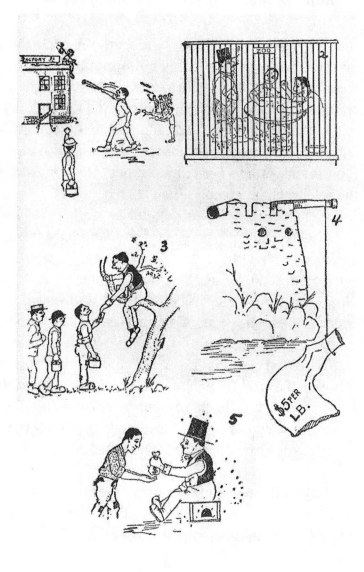

## 31. Laws of Memory—Association of Ideas

I remember vividly the autumn that the brunette pedagogue in charge of our village school commanded us to memorize the thirteen original states in the order in which they entered the Union.

I associated the facts and tied them together with the following story. Read this story twice and then see if you are not able to repeat the names of the celebrated thirteen in their correct order.

One Saturday afternoon a young lady from **Delaware** bought a ticket over the **Pennsylvania** railroad for a little outing. She packed a **New Jersey** sweater in her suitcase, and visited a friend, **Georgia**, in **Connecticut**. The next morning the hostess and her visitor attended **Mass** at **St. Mary's** Cathedral. After church they took the **South car line** home, and dined on **new ham**, which had been roasted by **Virginia**, the cook, from **New York**. After dinner they took the **North car line** and **rode** to the **island**.

You know from your own experience that it is much easier to remember a story than it is to retain in your mind a number of unrelated facts.

## 32. Laws of Memory—Repetition

Everyone is familiar with this principle. However, I have a few suggestions to offer you about repetition:

*a. Converse upon the points you want to memorize.*

Swing the conversation around as often as possible to the things that you want to fix in mind. That is the easiest method of repetition.

*b. The knowledge that repetition will fix a point in your memory is useless without action.*

Sooner or later every man discovers the astonishing fact that the only way to do a thing is *to do it*. It is useless to discuss the principle of repetition unless you apply it. Merely knowing what repetition will do, won't help your memory. You must act on that knowledge. The only way to repeat is—to repeat.

## 33. Laws of Memory—Depth of Impression

One minute of strict, alert attention will imbed a thing more deeply in your mind than will half and hour of half-hearted, indifferent thinking. Therefore it is easier to memorize when the birds are singing their matutinal songs than it is at vespers.

## 34. Memory and the Senses

If you hear a thing read you will impress it on your mind through the sense of sound. If you read it aloud yourself, you will impress it on your mind through two senses: the sense of sound and the sense of sight.

*So the best way to fix an outline in the mind is to write it down, look at it and read it aloud.*

Four

# Opening and Closing
# an Address

## 35. *Opening and Closing an Address*

*"Begin with a positive, concrete, striking statement. Tell them something at the start that will immediately grip their attention.*

*"Use short sentences. Try to make one word do the work of two.*

*"Finish strong. Daniel Webster tells us that he always worked out and memorized a strong closing sentence, no matter how extemporaneous the other portions of the speech might be. With a comprehensive outline and a strong closing sentence or paragraph the speaker is less likely to exceed the proper time.*

*"Many speeches otherwise effective have lost all effect because the speaker did not know when he was through. It is a matter of mere courtesy, both to the audience and to other speakers, to be as brief as logic and clearness allow. A college president, when asked by a visiting clergyman how long the latter could preach to the students, replied, 'There is no time limit, but rumor has it that no souls are saved after the first twenty minutes.'*

*"Finish strong and sharp."*

— U.S. Treasury's Handbook for
Liberty Loan Speakers

## 36. Importance of the Opening and Closing

The most important parts of an address are the beginning and the ending. The opening and closing remarks of an address are the most incisive and lasting.

## 37. Securing Favorable Attention

### a. Human Interest Story
One of the surest ways to get favorable attention is to tell a human interest story. We like to hear about other folks; that is why we read novels, see the movies, and discuss the neighbors.

### b. A Good Quotation
A good quotation is a splendid address-opener. It has two advantages: First, it has the same effect, in a lesser degree, as a human interest story—an infusion of warmth and personality; second, it adds force and begets confidence—especially when the person quoted is rated highly by the audience.

A speaker at the American Institute of Banking opened his Thrift talk with this surprising quotation:

"James J. Hill said: 'If you want to know whether you are going to succeed, the test is easy.

Are you able to save money? If not, drop out. You will surely lose. You may not think it, but you will lose as sure as you live.'"

### c. Begin on Common Ground

No matter how much you may differ with your auditors, you surely agree with them on some things. Begin by emphasizing the things you believe in common. That was Lincoln's plan. He emphasized the points on which all agreed and this convinced his opponents without their being conscious of it. Grant said of him: "He makes Stanton and Chase and the others feel that he is going their way, while all the time they are coming his."

So, begin on common ground. Reserve until later the things that you disagree about.

### 38. How to Begin a Speech

If your hearers are moving about and are noisy, just stand still and wait until they quiet down.

If you are in too big a hurry to begin, you show a lack of self-control. The suggestion you radiate is bad: it keeps you from winning confidence.

If there is too much noise, address your first remarks to the people nearest you. Begin in a simple, conversational manner. The others will become quiet in order to hear you.

## 39. Plans for Building a Speech

Divide your talk into blocks. Plan the opening and the closing of each block.

*a. Dr. Russell H. Conwell, the dean of American lecturers, builds his speeches like this:*
1. He secures favorable attention.
2. He states his facts.
3. He argues from them.
4. He appeals for action.

*b. Many speakers build their addresses on this plan:*
1. Show something that is wrong.
2. Show how to remedy it.
3. Appeal for action.

## 40. Ways to End an Address

The most important part of your address is its close. Your hearers usually will remember the points you made last better than any other parts of your talk.

Here are some ways to end an address:

*a. Know your closing almost word for word.*

*b. Sum up your point very briefly.*

Your audience cannot keep in mind all the point you have made. Sum them up rapidly. Summing up freshens them. It makes them stick.

*c. Be very clear and definite in your appeals for action. Tell your hearers exactly what to do and how to do it.*

*d. An illustration at the close of an address will drive your point home and make it easy to remember.*

Harrington Emerson closed his address on "The Cure of Wastes" with a concrete illustration:

"Franklin collected thirteen principles to cover the small amenities of daily life. They were: Temperance, silence, order, resolution, frugality, industry, sincerity, justice, moderation, cleanliness, tranquility, chastity, humility. Each week he picked out one and practiced it diligently, thus creating a habit. Each year he practiced each one a full week in each quarter, thus covering them all four times a year. He kept this up for many years. The uncouth Franklin of early manhood, who found fault with his wife for giving him a silver spoon and a china bowl for his bread and milk instead of a pewter spoon and an earthenware crock, developed into the statesman and man of the world who won the respect of the Englishmen, the admiration of Frenchmen, and the gratitude of Americans. In a similar way ought the principles of efficiency to be applied and reapplied."

Five

# *Preparing the Speech*

## 41. Preparing the Speech

*"Men give me some credit for genius. All the genius I have lies in this: When I have a subject in hand, I study it profoundly. Day and night it is before me. I explore it in all its bearings. My mind becomes pervaded with it. Then the effort which I make is what the people are pleased to call the fruits of genius. It is the fruit of labor and thought."* — Alexander Hamilton

*"What is it that first strikes us and strikes us at once, in a man of education, and which among educated men, so instantly distinguishes the man of superior mind? .... The true cause of the impression made upon us is that his mind is methodical."*
—S. T. Coleridge

*"Study carefully what you have to say, and put it into words in writing, or by speaking aloud to an imaginary person.*

*Arrange your points in order.*

*Stick to your order.*

*Divide your time among your points according to their importance.*

*Give each point the time you have appointed for it.*

*Stop when you are through."*
— Dr. Edward Everett Hale

## 42. Necessity for Thorough Preparation

It is just as ridiculous to try to get thoughts out of your head when they are not there—to speak without being prepared—as it is to draw checks on a bank where you have no account.

You can't fake preparation; half knowledge and vague impressions will only make your speech back-fire and pop and stall.

And another thing: know a great deal more than you expect to use.

When I was hunting coyotes one winter up on the plains of South Dakota, we found ourselves twenty miles from home and gasoline—and there was just one little gallon of fuel in the tank of our Chevrolet. The range horses were playing and the steers were sniffing the air. A regular old north-western blizzard was sweeping from the Black Hills eastward, and we knew it might mean an under-taker's bill if we didn't get in. We had enough gas to take us home, but we felt pretty shaky on the last lap of the trip, listening for the engine to start sputtering and missing. If we had had a couple of extra gallons along we wouldn't have used them, but I'll tell you if we could have known they were there if we needed them, it would have been infi-nitely comforting. It would have boosted our stock of confidence and self-reliance. Catch the idea, don't you? When you start making an address, have a reserve supply of material to draw on—prepare more than you expect to use.

## 43. *Analyzing the Speech*

Take some matter affecting your business, or some matter affecting your social group, or your town. If you prefer, choose some national problem. Think it out deliberately, as if the responsibility for decision rested upon you. Answer the question: What does this plan mean? What is involved in deciding this way or that? What will be the effect? Draw up the statement in writing, on three sheets of paper. And be sure to express everything in definite, complete sentences—as you talk—not in mere phrases.

At the head of the first sheet write: *What does this plan mean?* Below write your answer, making it as clear and complete as you can.

At the head of the second sheet write the question: *What are the reasons against it?* Below set down in the same manner all the reasons which you can think of against the proposal.

Now place the second and third sheets side by side and compare them. What statements or assertions *cancel out?* What remains on each side? Where does the balance lie?

## 44. An Example of Speech Analysis

Suppose, for example, the proposal is made to permit the employees of a company to share a part of its profits; imagine yourself to have the responsibility of deciding. You might draw up a balance sheet of the reasons for an against, as follows:

### a. What Does the Plan Involve?

1. All employees of the company shall receive a share of the profits as a part of their remuneration.

2. Present salaries not to be cut but all future raises in salaries to be given in the form of a share of the company's profits.

3. The profit-sharing awards are to be computed and distributed quarterly.

### b. Reasons in Favor of the Plan

1. Will give men extra incentive to speed up production.

2. Will cause employees to take interest and pride in their tasks: it is a well-known fact that men are more interested in working for themselves than in working for others and under this new system every employee of the company will, to a certain extent, be working for himself.

3. Ought to reduce labor troubles by making

workmen more contented.

4. Ought to enable company to keep employees longer. Employees will not want to quit until the end of the quarter when their profit-sharing compensation can be computed.

5. Ought to help employees save, as their increases in salary will be saved for them automatically until the end of the quarter.

6. Ought to increase company's profits, as it will make workmen more economical and speed up production.

7. Has worked well with certain companies (name them).

*c. Reasons against Plan*

1. Will necessitate extra labor in bookkeeping department to ascertain company's profits quarterly.

2. Will make knowledge of company's profits public information which will undoubtedly come into the possession of competitors.

3. It will be difficult to fix the exact percentage of profits that each class of workmen will receive. If the percentage is too low, it will defeat the whole purpose of the plan. If it is too high, it will reduce the company's profits out of the proper proportion.

4. It will entail hardship on some employees to wait until the end of the quarter to receive the

profit-sharing portion of their remuneration.

5. It may encourage reckless spending. Some of the employees, finding themselves at the end of the quarter in the possession of an extra few hundred dollars or so, may be tempted to squander it immediately on unwarranted luxuries.

6. It may increase labor troubles. Workmen will be contented when the profits are large, but many of them will not be willing to curtail their expenses during periods when the company's profits are small or negligible.

7. It may be more costly than ordinary increases in wages. An employee may be contented with a small addition to his wage but if his additional remuneration from profit sharing is small it is likely to defeat its very purpose; on the other hand, if it is large enough to accomplish its object, it is very probable that it will be more costly than wage increases.

8. Has worked badly in certain companies (name them).

### d. Striking a Balance

The case may be summarized as follows:

1. Plan will give men extra incentive to economize and increase production. This heightened loyalty ought to increase the company's profits, but the plan will necessitate extra expense. It will probably mean more income for the employ-

ees than they would receive in salary increases. As to whether or not the extra profits will offset the extra expenses, it is difficult to say.

2. It will encourage some men to save, others to spend recklessly—depending upon the individual. It should make men more contented, but it may have the opposite effect in stringent times.

3. It may work hardship on some employees.

4. It is going to be difficult to fix the exact ratio.

5. It is going to make some of our business secrets public information.

6. It has worked well with some corporation and badly with others.

*e. Verdict*

Plan should be given trial. In order to prevent employees from spending their awards recklessly at the end of each quarter, they should be urged to purchase company's stock.


*45. Methods of Well-Known Speakers*

When John H. Patterson, President of the National Cash Register Company, talks to his men, he uses a great pad of paper mounted on an artist's easel, so that he can draw pictures and diagrams. If he analyzes a problem with his audience, he draws beam scales, and lists on one side the advantages and on the other side the objections to any certain plan. This shows the reasons for and against, in their true proportions. When speaking before small groups try this device; it will make your argument as clear as a mountain lake—and incidentally it will help you to hold their attention and interest, too.

~ ~ ~

The simplest and most naïve method of outlining a speech which I have ever heard, was suggested to me by reading one of Dr. Edward Everett Hale's books. He says a speaker should write to a friend and say, "I am to make an address on a certain subject and I want to make these points. He should then enumerate the things he is going to speak about in their correct order."

"If he finds he has nothing to say in his letter," continues Dr. Hale, "he had better write to the committee that invited him, and say that the probable death of his grandmother will possibly prevent his being present on the occasion."

~ ~ ~

When I make notes for a speech, I jot things down in whatever order they occur to me—main ideas, illustrations, concrete instances, etc. And—this is very important—I use a separate card or page of my pocket notebook for each idea.

Ideas may come to me slowly at first, but the longer I work the more rapidly they tumble out of my brain. You will undoubtedly have the same experience.

Now I spread out in front of me my cards or the leaves from my notebook and play solitaire with them. Suppose I am speaking on the value of studying public speaking. Eight of my notes may deal with the mental value of such training—all right, I place them on top of one another. Perhaps fifteen more deal with the commercial value of good address and self-confidence—all right, I put all of them in another place. In this fashion I soon have all my notes in three or four stacks which constitute the main divisions of my address. Then I play solitaire with each of these groups by itself and subdivide it into smaller groups; this gives me my subdivisions.

This simple manner of planning an address is used by some of the most successful speakers in the United States. I heartily commend it.

## 46. "Reader's Guide to Periodical Literature"

You should make extensive use of the "Reader's Guide to Periodical Literature."

This can be found in every library, and, to a

speaker, it is indispensable. It lists in alphabetical order all of the magazine articles that have appeared.

When I prepared an address on Strikes, I found indexed under the heading in the "Reader's Guide to Periodical Literature," all the magazine articles dealing with that subject that had appeared during the last twenty years. I picked out those that my time permitted me to read, procured the back issues of these magazines from the librarian, and I had at my disposal the well-digested thoughts of the best writers on this subject. In this manner I was able to pack my address with specific instances and concrete illustrations to back up my assertions.

## 47. The Note-Taking Habit

Early in life I formed the invaluable habit of making notes.

Thoughts and illustrations are as elusive as partridges, so I wing them the moment they rise out of the grass, and salt them down in my notebook larder.

Felix Arnold, the psychologist, says in his book, *Attention and Interest*: "Remember that about half the new matter presented is forgotten after the first half hour, two-thirds in nine hours, three-quarters after six days, and four-fifths after a month."

So you see if one wants to retain his mental impressions he has to rope and hog-tie them.

I am following pretty good examples in this notebook business; Lowell, Hawthorne, Webster, Phillips Brooks, Emerson, and others of their mental caliber, used notebooks all their lives.

~ ~ ~

I not only make notes in a little book which I always carry in my hip pocket, but whenever I read a magazine, I make copious notes on the margins and underline the particularly helpful passages: perhaps it is a new combination of words, such as "yeasty ideas," or "it was so quiet that the silence fairly shrieked"; perhaps it is a good story, a striking illustration, a dynamic thought or fact.

No magazine that contains anything I like is ever thrown away; each article read is noted in my card-index file under a general heading.

I use large, yellow manila envelopes as files, each marked for some subject on my list. Clippings from newspapers and magazines and notes made at various times, are placed in the proper envelopes.

## 48. A Foundation of Knowledge

You must have a foundation of clear reliable

knowledge and know a subject like the back of your hand before you can cut loose and do yourself credit.

This is one of the chief points to remember in gaining confidence: know thoroughly what you want to say.

Socrates said that men could be eloquent on any subject that they understood.

My experience has taught me that the best things about your speeches are—you. You are preparing speeches all the time by storing up ideas and impressions and experiences.

One Friday night I made a painfully mediocre address before my debating society on the subject of Foreign Immigration. Later that evening I was called upon quite unexpectedly for an impromptu talk on cowboys. And to my surprise, my impromptu effort was infinitely better than my prepared one. Why? Well, I had read for an hour about Foreign Immigration, and had had no time to digest or assimilate the impressions I had gleaned. I really wasn't prepared on the subject at all. But cowboys! I had lived for three years in the cow country of Wyoming and Dakota; I spoke from genuine, first-hand impressions—the finest kind of preparation.

Everyone is prepared by his experience to talk well on some subject.

# Six

# *Making Your Meaning Clear*

## 49. Making Your Meaning Clear

"*My father was a man of great intellectual energy. My best training came from him. He was intolerant of vagueness, and from the time I began to write until his death in 1903, when he was eighty-one years old, I carried everything I wrote to him. He would make me read it aloud, which was always painful to me. Every now and then he would stop me. 'What do you mean by that?' I would tell him, and, of course, in doing so would express myself more simply than I had on paper. 'Why didn't you say so?' he would go on. 'Don't shoot at your meaning with birdshot and hit the whole countryside; shoot with a rifle at the thing you have to say.'*" — Woodrow Wilson

## 50. Talk in Terms of Your Hearers' Experience

Suppose you were delivering a travel talk and wanted to make your audience realize the height of the Great Pyramid. An encyclopedia will tell you 451 feet, but your audience won't get an accurate picture of a building expressed in feet. The Woolworth Building lifts upward 756 feet; so if you were addressing New Yorkers you could say, "The Great Pyramid is a little more than half as high as the Woolworth Tower." Describe the Great Pyramid so that the people in your town can see its height.

A group of missionaries wanted to translate this verse for an African tribe:

"Though your sins be as scarlet, they shall be as white as snow."

But these tribesmen of the tropics had never snowballed one another or scooped off the sidewalks on February mornings; so they knew no more about snow than they knew about the monoaceticacidester of salicylic acid. But they had climbed cocoanut trees many times; so the missionaries changed the verse to read:

"Though your sins be as scarlet, they shall be as white as the meat of a cocoanut."

In order to make the other fellow understand, you have to draw your illustrations from things he knows about. Apply this principle in your conversation, your letter-writing, your advertising, and your public addresses. Talk to the other man in terms with which he is entirely familiar.

## 51. Talk in Terms of Your Listener's Point of View

Adapt yourself to the other man, and his way of looking at things.

A shrewd life insurance salesman doesn't begin by talking about the strength of his company, and the fact that it has been in business since McClellan's men charged the flame-swept fields of Antietam. The prospect is not interested yet in the strength of the success of some big company. He is, however, intensely concerned about himself, and so the shrewd canvasser either shows him that life insurance is a splendid investment or informs him that almost ninety percent of adults leave no estate at death. He tells him that death would throw his wife and little girls upon charity for support. He talks life insurance from his hearer's side, until the prospect asks how much the premium on ten thousand will cost.

Then he may be interested in knowing something of the strength of the company he intends to patronize.

## 52. Use of Drawings

Listeners are hit hardest, as a rule, when their sense of sight is appealed to. Then why not actually draw a picture illustrating a point? The next time you talk—either in public or in private—on any subject that *can* be illustrated, use exhibits, or *drawings*. They will attract attention, stimulate interest, and make clear your meaning. A knack of free-hand drawing, no matter how rough, is a decided asset.

## 53. How One Man Attained Clearness

John D. Rockefeller, Jr. tells how he obtained clearness in addressing laborers by appealing to their sense of sight:

"I found that they (the employees of the Colorado Fuel and Iron Co.) imagined the Rockefellers had been drawing immense profits from their interests in Colorado; no end of people had told them so. I explained the exact situation to them. I showed them that during the fourteen years in which we had been connected with the Colorado Fuel and Iron Co., it had never paid one cent in dividends upon the common stock.

"At one of the meetings, I gave a practical illustration of the finances of the company. I put a number of coins on the table. I swept off a portion which represented their wages—for the first claim upon the company is the pay roll. Then I took away more coins to represent the salaries of the officers, and then the remaining coins to represent the fees of the directors. There were no coins left for the stockholders. And then I asked: 'Men, is it fair, in this corporation where we are all partners, that three of the partners should get all the earnings, be they large or small—all of them—and the fourth nothing?'

"After the illustration, one of the men made a speech for higher wages. I asked him, 'Is it fair for you to want more wages when one of the partners gets nothing?' He admitted that it did not look like a square deal; I heard no more about increasing the wages."

## 54. Word Pictures

Make your appeal to the eye definite and specific. For instance, the word "dog" calls up a more or less definite picture of such an animal— perhaps a cocker spaniel, a Scotch terrier, a St. Bernard, or a Pomeranian. Notice how much more distinct an image springs into your mind when I say "bulldog"—the term is less inclusive. "A brindle bulldog," calls up a still more explicit picture.

Similarly, it is more graphic to say "a black Shetland pony" than to talk of a "a horse"; "a white bantam rooster with a broken leg" gives a much more precise image than "fowl."

## 55. Use of Specific Instances

General assertions by themselves are too vague to be either clear or convincing. You will be understood much more readily if you will back up your assertions with specific instances illustrating your point. I shall take my own medicine and illustrate the use of specific instances with a specific instance. I heard a speaker declare that the men in control of big business lead simple lives. That statement didn't convey much to his hearers; they didn't know enough about the living habits of our colonels of industry to realize what he meant. The next time he delivered that address, he clarified his statement with these nine specific instances:

John D. Rockefeller had a leather couch in his office at 26 Broadway, and made it a steel-riveted rule to take a midday nap.

J. Ogden Armour retires at nine o'clock, and is up again at six.

George F. Baker, who is the dominating factor in more corporations than any other man living, has never tasted a cocktail. He began to smoke only a few years ago.

John H. Patterson, President of the National Cash Register Company, neither smokes nor drinks.

Frank Vanderlip, until recently president of the largest bank in America, eats only two meals a day.

Milk and old-fashioned ginger wafers often constituted Harriman's midday meal.

Jacob H. Schiff delights to lunch on a glass of milk.

Andrew Carnegie's favorite dish is oatmeal and cream.

What effect did these specific instances have on your mind? They are interesting, aren't they? And they make the general statement easy to understand and believe, don't they? Remember that specific instances produce largely the same impression on other people as they produce on you.

When you converse in private or speak in public, shun generalities. You will be surprised to find how the habit of being concrete and specific will make you a clearer and more interesting speaker.

## 56. Avoid Technical Terms

If you belong to a profession the work of which is technical—if you are a lawyer, a physician, an engineer, or are in a highly specialized line of business—be doubly careful when you talk to outsiders, to express yourself in plain terms, to give necessary details. To illustrate: A physician remarked in a public address that "diaphragmatic breathing is a great aid to health." He was perfectly clear to himself and to the half dozen physicians in the audience; but few of his hearers knew how or why diaphragmatic breathing is superior to chest breathing. His words did not convey to his auditors what they meant to himself. When his attention was called to the obscurity, he clarified his statement by adding these details:

"The diaphragm is a thin muscle forming the floor of the chest at the base of the lungs and the roof of the abdominal cavity. When inactive and during chest breathing, it is arched like an inverted washbowl.

"In abdominal breathing every breath forces this muscular arch down until it becomes nearly flat and you can feel your stomach muscles pressing against your belt. This downward pressure of the diaphragm massages and stimulates the organs of the upper part of the abdominal cavity—the stomach, the liver, the pancreas, the spleen, the solar plexus.

"When you breathe out again your stomach and your intestines will be forced up against the diaphragm and will be given another massage. This massaging helps the process of elimination.

"A vast amount of ill health originates in the intestines. Most indigestion, constipation, and auto-intoxication would disappear if our stomachs and intestines were properly exercised through deep forcible breathing."

## 57. Arrange Your Ideas in an Orderly Way

Group together your facts. When you start one phase of a subject, finish it before going to the next. I advised you previously to put your notes on separate pieces of paper and then play solitaire with them. Such a plan helps you materially to group together your related facts.

Arrange the various divisions of your speech so that each one leads logically to the next. This method will make it far easier for you to remember your outline. It will also make your talk simpler to listen to. It will make its logic more invincible.

## 58. Use the Climax

In presenting a series of ideas, place the most striking one last.

A classic illustration of the anti-climax is the phrase: "For God, for country, and for Yale." These words, of course, are mentioned in the inverse order of their importance. Probably the best known illustration of the climax is Caesar's famous message: "I came, I saw, I conquered."

Herbert Spencer in his splendid little book, *The Philosophy of Style*, explains the necessity for the climax:

"As immediately after looking at the sun we cannot perceive the light of a fire, while by looking at the fire first and the sun afterwards we can perceive both; so, after receiving a brilliant, or weighty, or terrible thought, we cannot appreciate a less brilliant, less weighty, less terrible one, while, by reversing the order, we can appreciate each."

Seven

# *The Convincing Speech*

## 59. The Convincing Speech

"If I should reduce my principles of idea-conveying to a creed, it would run something in this fashion:

1. The nerves from the eyes to the brain are many times larger than those from the ears to the brain. Therefore, when possible to use a picture instead of words, use one and make the words mere connections for the picture.

2. Confine the attention to the exact subject by drawing outlines and putting in the divisions; then we make certain that we are all talking about the same thing.

3. Aim for dramatic effects either in speaking or writing—study them out beforehand. This holds the attention.

4. Red is the best color to attract and hold attention, therefore use plenty of it.

5. Few words—short sentences, small words—big ideas.

6. Tell why as well as how.

7. Do not be afraid of big type and do not put too much on a page.

8. Do not crowd ideas in speaking or writing. No advertisement is big enough for two ideas.

9. Before you try to convince anyone else, make sure that you are convinced, and if you cannot convince yourself, drop the subject. Do not

*try to 'put over anything.'*
    *10. Tell the truth."*
    — John H. Patterson, President,
        National Cash Register Co.

## 60. The Human Interest Appeal

Alden, in his "Art of Debate," quotes a speaker who stirred his audience to enthusiasm by adding this little human interest touch to his speech:

"If necessary, every regiment in the United States Army must be called out, that the letter dropped by the girl Jennie, at some country post office back in Maine, may go on its way to her lover in San Francisco without a finger being raised to stop its passage."

Suppose the speaker had merely said that the troops should be called out, if necessary, to prevent interference with the mails. Wouldn't such a flat statement have been infinitely less impressive than the human interest reference to Jennie and her lover?

Whenever possible, show how your proposition affects the vital interests and feelings of human beings.

## 61. Use of Concrete Illustrations

Go straight to the point. Cite concrete illustrations, in order that we shall know better what you are talking about. Use a whole battery of specific instances.

Now to illustrate. Suppose I say to you:

"Young man, shun debts. They will worry you and hold you back. One of England's greatest statesmen, Benjamin Disraeli, tells in his diary how he hesitated to accept an invitation to speak to a banquet for fear he should be nabbed for debt when he arose to respond to his toast."

Good, so far: but you are neither impressed nor convinced, are you? Why? Well, I have not cited enough illustrations to drive my point home. Suppose I continue:

"Balzac, the famous novelist, was a slave to debt. This great genius was afraid to pause in his labors for a single day. He would write from two o'clock in the morning until late at night again in order to stave off his creditors. The story of how he toiled under his great financial burdens is one of the most pathetic I know. Men like Cicero, William IV, Bret Harte, Eugene Field, and Mark Twain had their lives poisoned by the misery of debt. They managed to be great but no man knows how much greater and happier their careers might have been, had they not been hampered by debts."

Has the piling up of these specific instances impressed you?

When you argue by illustration you state things indirectly. You imply more than you say. Your statements are hard to challenge. It is one of the most powerful, if not the most powerful kind of argument.

## 62. Restating an Assertion in Different Phrases

If I don't have several specific instances, I can get somewhat the same effect by restating my assertion in different phrases.

Listen to this: Sydney Smith advances only one idea in these three sentences. He phrases the same thought in different ways until it is driven deep into your mind:

"A great deal of talent is lost in the world for the want of a little courage. Every day sends to their graves obscure men whom timidity prevented from making a first effort; who, if they could have been induced to begin, would in all probability have gone great lengths in the career of fame. The fact is, that to do anything in the world worth doing, we must not stand back, shivering, and thinking of the cold and danger, but jump in and scramble through as well as we can."

I have seen this method used hundreds of

times in addresses, advertisements, and sales literature. However, there is such a thing as over-doing it and tiring your hearers. Use this principle with judgment and taste.

## 63. *Value of Analogy*

Let us see how Lincoln argued by analogy. He was replying to the critics of his war policy:

"Gentlemen, I want you to suppose a case for a moment. Suppose that all the property you were worth was in gold, and you had put it in the hands of Blondin, the famous rope-walker, to carry across the Niagara Falls on a tight rope. Would you shake the rope while he was passing over it, or keep shouting to him, 'Blondin, stoop a little more! Go a little faster!' No, I am sure you would not. You would hold your breath as well as your tongue, and keep your hand off until he was safely over. Now, the Government is in the same situation. It is carrying an immense weight across the stormy ocean. Untold treasures are in its hands. It is doing the best it can. Don't badger it! Just keep still and it will get you safely over."

Convincing, isn't it? Hard to challenge too.

## 64. Value of Numbers

It is hard for you and me to realize the cumulative value of small sums. We break a ten dollar bill, do a little shopping, and are surprised to find that it has disappeared so rapidly. We don't realize how quickly small sums added together, mount up into a large total. When you want to make a large sum seem small, reverse the process. Break it up into small bits. A life insurance salesman wanted to impress his hearers with the cheapness of the commodity he was selling, so he said:

"A man below thirty can at death leave his family one thousand dollars by cutting out his daily five cent shoe-shine, doing the job himself, and investing the sum saved in insurance. A man of thirty-four who smokes a quarter's worth of cigars daily can stay with his family longer, and leave his dependents three thousand dollars more, by spending his Havana money for insurance."

Of course, you would reverse your tactics to get the opposite effect. You can make small sums appear huge by massing them. That is what the New York Telephone Company did in this announcement:

"Out of each one hundred telephone connections made, nearly seven show a delay of more than a minute before the person called answers. Every day 140,000 minutes are lost in this way. In the course of a year, this minute's delay in New York is about equal to all the business days that have elapsed since Columbus discovered America."

## 65. How to Appeal to the Reason

Before you attempt to convince anyone else, test your opinions by such questions as these:

1. Why do I believe so and so?

2. Am I believing a thing because I want it to be true or do the facts warrant my belief?

3. Have I arrived at my conclusions with insufficient data? What facts have I to warrant my belief?

4. Are the instances from which I am forming my judgment, typical or abnormal?

5. If I am taking the word of someone else, is he in a position to know what he is speaking about and is he biased?

When you are absolutely sure that you are right, when you know you are *right* and *feel* it in your heart, you can convince the other fellow with half the effort you would otherwise require.

## 66. How to Appeal to the Feelings

To impress people, you must stir their

feelings.

Suppose I were to tell you that people lived until a few centuries ago without some of our most common articles of food, without the convenience of adequate communication or transportation, without our medical knowledge.

I shouldn't impress you very much, should I? No—too vague and general.

But if I talked about everyday things which you *feel* about—suppose I said:

"People lived without sugar until the thirteenth century, without coal till the fourteenth, without butter till the fifteenth, without tobacco and potatoes till the sixteenth, without tea, coffee, and soap till the seventeenth, without lamps till the eighteenth, without trains, telegrams, gas, matches, and chloroform till the nineteenth, without automobiles, wireless, or aeroplanes until the twentieth."

Don't you feel the difference when we get down to brass bushings and things you *feel* about?

## 67. How to Appeal to the Senses

It is not enough to stir one of the feelings; you must drive home your point from every angle possible. You have five senses: touching, tasting, smelling, hearing, and seeing. Try to strike through all five. Hit then all and hit them hard, and you will make deep impressions.

Here is a soldier's story. Note how he stirs several of your senses.

"When I came to I was in a shell hole. There was the taste of hot blood in my mouth.

"Felt something hard on my tongue, and I rolled over and spit out some of my teeth.

"It was an old battlefield and the stench of men and horses rotting in the July sun was nauseating.

"I heard the screams of the wounded, and the tattoo of machine guns. One man was calling for his mother. Another was calling to God.

"The man next to be had been bayoneted, and I could see his bloody entrails in the sunlight."

## 68. Appeal to the Sense of Sight

Most people are more impressed by what they see than by what they hear. All of us have the experience of remembering people's faces when we cannot recall their names. Whenever possible, therefore, appeal to the sense of sight. The same things which were said previously in praise of appealing to the eye through pictures and drawings and exhibits in order to obtain clearness, could well be repeated here. To be impressive and convincing, appeal to the eye by every means possible and at every opportunity.

## 69. How to Quote Authorities

Try to quote some eminent authority to back up your assertions. Most people won't think of questioning the judgment of an eminent man. The bigger the man, the more impressive is his testimony. However, even the testimony of unknown people often has a telling effect. Think how commonly it is used in advertising.

### a. Be Definite

Don't say, "Authorities on this subject maintain." Who are your authorities? Name them. Are you ashamed of them? Don't you know who they are? Then how do you know what they said?

Don't declare that "Many prominent men believe." If many prominent men hold the view you are presenting, why not reveal the identities of a few of them?

Don't begin, "Statistics show." What statistics? Who gathered the statistics and when and for what purpose?

Of course, it is permissible to quote one authority and to add that "Cornelius Blank and Gregory Justin and many other authorities of equal eminence hold the same view." It is impossible to quote many authorities verbatim. In quoting authorities remember these things.

### b. Quote a Popular Authority
We are much more likely to be influenced by someone we like.

### c. Quote an Authority in Whom Your Hearers Have Confidence
A man is usually most impressed by testimony from authorities in his own profession—attorneys by members of the bar, business men by commercial executives, and so on.

### d. Be Sure That Your Authority Is in a Position to Give Expert Testimony
A few years ago a tobacco firm used placards in the New York street cars telling what George M. Cohan and other well-known Gothamites thought of that brand of smoking tobacco. I imagine that the campaign produced results, for the public at large is very much impressed with the testimony of well-known men, but the people who have a cerebrum and a cerebellum functioning are not taken in by that sort of testimony. George M. Cohan is a splendid playwright and actor and composer of Broadway songs, but do those characteristics qualify him as a better judge of smoking tobacco

than any other smoker whose financial budget enables him to cull out the most satisfying brand? Of course not.

### e. Be Sure That Your Authority Is Not Prejudiced

I am quite positive that Mr. Cohan was handsomely rewarded for all the encomiums he heaped upon this particular brand of smoking tobacco. Is it possible that this remuneration colored and warped his judgment?

In quoting authority, be sure that your authority is not biased or prejudiced.

### f. Quote Local Authorities

A Philadelphia audience will, as a general rule, be more readily convinced by the assertions of an authority living in their city, one they know or can investigate, than by the statements of a citizen of San Antonio—regardless of the prophet-without-honor-in-his-own-home principle.

### 70. Truth and Sincerity are Impressive and Convincing

I have seen many speakers whose talks sprang not from a deep, genuine sincerity that was welling up within them; but from a desire to make an impression and put something over on the other fellow. Every man who has hired salesmen has discovered men who thought that all they had to have were a few samples and a superficial knowledge of the product and a mileage book. These men didn't realize that their own inner feelings, that their own attitudes toward the things they were saying and the men they were trying to sell are powers—powers as real as sunlight and shadow.

If you try to convince others of things that you don't firmly and sincerely believe, you will meet the fate that you deserve. Your hearers may not know why you are not impressive and convincing; but they will *feel* that you are not.

Truth will make you aggressive and convincing. When a man speaks from a deep, genuine conviction, he unconsciously appears frank and sincere and above board. The audience somehow feels these qualities and they have confidence in the man who radiates them. Sincerity and truth are vital and dynamic. They are as much of a force and as real as the electricity by which you read your evening paper.

Eight

# *The Humorous Speech*

## 71. The Humorous Speech

*"If I were giving advice to the fellow who is starting in the humor writing game, I should tell him to forget all that "guff" about having to be born with a sense of humor in order to succeed. That, as the Latins have so tersely put it, is all BUSHWAH. Nearly everybody is born with a sense of humor."*

—*Irvin S. Cobb*

## 72. Why People Laugh

Most humor is based on a feeling of superiority or egotism. I don't mean that only egotistical people laugh, but—well, let me illustrate:

A fat man is walking down the street with his head turned back in a determined effort to see the tops of the skyscrapers when he steps on a banana peel and, waving his arms in a frantic effort to clutch the unoffending atmosphere, sits abruptly and reverberatingly down.

The spectators laugh because they feel superior to the fat man. They feel that if they were going down the street, they would watch out and would not step on the tropical fruit-peel with such catastrophic results.

Of course, we don't laugh where there is a misfortune. If the fat man hurts himself in his fall we cease laughing and telephone for the ambulance.

~ ~ ~

It tickles our egotism when we see others placed in an embarrassing situation—and we laugh. Charlie Chaplin says:

"The one point of human nature that I play upon more than anything...is that it strikes people as funny when they see someone else placed in an undignified and embarrassing situation.

"One of the things most quickly learned in theatrical work is that people as a whole get satisfaction from seeing the rich get the worst of things. The reason for this, of course, lies in the fact that nine-tenths of the people in the world are poor, and secretly resent the wealth of the other tenth."

Most stories that bring a laugh are based on a feeling on the part of the audience that its members would know better than to be similarly situated. Audiences especially like stories of people above them wherein the leading character—some millionaire or a nobleman—is made to appear in a ridiculous light. An audience likes to have its ego tickled. The successful public speakers are the ones who know how to apply the feather.

## 73. Particularize Your Protagonist

In mentioning your protagonist, particularize. Don't say a lord and let it go at that. Give him a monocle, imitate his talk. Vivify him before going on with the story. Then the audience sees some definite character; when the point of the story comes and the character has his downfall, then the audience has something specific and definite to laugh at.

## 74. Telling a Joke on Yourself

A joke that a speaker tells on himself is much better than one told on somebody else. The audience is interested in the speaker: it is not in John Jones.

Don't hesitate to tell a story of how you got the worst of it in a horse trade, or of when you bought a second-hand automobile, or of what happened the first time you put on a dress suit and went to see a girl. The more the audience laughs at you while you are telling the story, the more they will like you later.

Of course this feature could be overdone. A speaker must preserve his dignity.

## 75. The Varieties of Humor

If a big thing is understated, we laugh because we see the false value. People laughed when Mark Twain said that the report of his death was "greatly exaggerated"; they saw that he had understated a thing and it tickled them.

~ ~ ~

For platform purposes, exaggeration and

overstatement are better than understatement. They can be grasped more easily. It is best to have a short story leading up to only one point.

Harry Kelly, an actor, used to tell this one with splendid effect:

"A farmer's daughter bought some raisin buns at a small town bakery. She found a fly in one and took back the bun and made a kick. The baker said, 'If you'll bring back the fly, I'll give you a raisin.'"

~ ~ ~

A pun is not a high order of humor. It is based on the double meaning of a word. To illustrate:

Someone asked Chauncey Depew if life was worth living. He said it depended on the liver.

The reader gets a sense of delight on hearing that, for he realizes that he is clever enough to see two meanings in the last word, and capable enough to know what the narrator meant.

## 76. Use of Humorous Stories

Humor is a very delicate thing, and it must be time accurately or it may fail to explode.

Eliminate all superfluous words.

Make your stories short: the long ones usually misfire.

Don't drag in long stories apropos of nothing: it is permissible in after-dinner addresses to be funny for the mere sake of being funny, but if you are attempting a dignified address, let humor be the sauce of the meal—not the meat.

Don't drag in a story by the hair of its head. If you are talking about salesmanship and see that the attention of your audience is waning, don't suddenly stop and change your voice and tell a Pullman porter story. Let the porter sleep; let him sleep unless he fits into the mood of the occasion.


## 77. When to Tell Humorous Stories

Humorous touches will rest an audience in a serious address and sometimes will drive home a point infinitely better than preaching.

Too often the public speaker tries to open up with a humorous story, believing that once he makes the audience laugh, he has it with him. Such is not always the case. The audience usually feels that the speaker is making overtures too quickly. Nine times out of ten the introductory humorous story has written all over it that it is dragged in.

It is usually better to begin on a serious note, and let the audience get acquainted with your looks and with your manner of expression; and then, after mutual confidence has been established, to tell them a humorous anecdote. Strickland Gillilan, the greatest humorous lecturer in the United States, makes it a point not to tell a humorous story the first three minutes he is on the platform.

Edward James Cattell, the noted Philadelphia after-dinner speaker, advises speakers to end their addresses on a serious note.

We love to laugh, but life is not a joke, and a speaker should leave something worthwhile ringing in the ears of his auditors.

Nine

# *The Well-Delivered Speech*

## 78. The Well-Delivered Speech

*"How many people owe their advancement, their position, largely to their ability to talk well! Making a good appearance, a favorable first impression, is everything, and no one can do this so well as a charming talker....How many men in public life owe their success and popularity largely to their fine conversational powers....Many a man has talked himself into a good position and a fine salary, when his ability alone would never have carried him there."* — Dr. Orison Swett Marden

*"...the simplest man with passion is more persuasive than the most eloquent without it."*
— La Rochefoucauld

*The public speaker must "set forth with power and attractiveness the very same topics which others discuss in such tame and bloodless phraseology."* — Cicero

## 79. Importance of Good Delivery

No man who desires to maintain a reputation for possessing common sense would disparage the importance of logical speech construction and sound argument, but we must admit that the old adage is true—*"It is not so much what you say as how you say it."*

I have watched competing speakers hundreds of times, in everything from college debates to business arguments and political campaigns, and I have noticed that the man with the more persuasive delivery almost invariably wins, even though his opponent is more logical.

Look well, therefore, to your delivery.

The secret of good delivery is amazingly simple. It is not easy to apply, strange to say, but its basic principle can be grasped by a child.

Why it is not more generally understood and practiced by speakers is an enigma to me.

Many books have enshrouded it with mystery and engulfed it in theories.

## 80. Secret of Good Delivery

Not one man in ten thousand is able without drill or practice to attain enlarged naturalness and carry it to the platform. *Yet that is the secret of effective speaking: enlarged naturalness.*

Let the man who converses with you in a colorful, emphatic, and convincing manner—let that man mount the platform and face an audience, and the chances are a hundred to one that he will instantly lose his naturalness, become stilted, speak in a monotonous tone. He becomes mechanical and draws back into his shell like a snapping turtle.

Just why that sad transformation should take place—well, who can say? I am only recording the fact; not endeavoring to explain it.

## 81. Exceptions Which Test the Rule

I have said that the secret of good delivery is enlarged naturalness, but, of course, there are exceptions which test the rule. For instance, if a man stutters in conversation or drops off the *g* from words ending in *ing*, or if he naturally converses in a frightened manner or in a blustering way—under such conditions, of course, enlarged naturalness will enlarge these faults. Many men need to eliminate certain errors which have crept into their manner of conversing. In a book of this kind one naturally has to deal with rules, not with individual exceptions; so I reaffirm that *as a general thing the secret of good delivery is enlarged naturalness.*

## 82. Developing Self-Expression

Perhaps you have a little boy or girl at home. When your child becomes angry, he expresses himself splendidly, doesn't he? He hasn't required a course in public speaking to train him to express his thoughts and feelings.

You, yourself, are also a very effective speaker when you are talking to some of the members of your family—especially if you are under the influence of your feelings so that you have forgotten yourself and let yourself go. You let down your guards then, don't you, and talk in a natural and telling manner? Most people do.

## 83. Some Practice Drills

If you think it is easy to be natural, read aloud the following short selections for practice. Ask a friend to shut his eyes and listen to you.

Does he says that it sounds like natural conversation, or a declamation, or a prepared speech?

To practice delivering these colloquial sentences is splendid drill; for it drives home the necessity for *enlarged naturalness*.

You are urged to turn to this lesson frequently and drill yourself in the simple, natural speaking of these conversational statements.

## ADMISSION
Of course, there is something after all to be said in his favor.

Well, now that I come to think of it, I believe you are right at that.

## ANGER
Stop it! Now, I've had enough out of you. He's a liar and he doesn't dare deny it.

## APPEAL
Now, listen, please. Have a heart. How would you want to be treated if you were in my place?

I beg of you to help. These people are old and aged and helpless—and hungry. Suppose it were your old father or your old mother.

## APPROVAL
Fine! That's great! Where did you get it?

Congratulations, old man! Corking good speech. You put it across, believe me!

## APOLOGY
I'm sorry. Honestly, I am. I wouldn't have hurt you for anything in the world.

I apologize. I'm wrong. I admit it.

## ARGUMENT

That's ridiculous! He never meant that—and you know it. If he had intended to come, why didn't he write?

Reason? I'm willing to listen to it when I hear any. But abuse isn't reason. You haven't done anything but call him names. That's not getting us anywhere. Now let's get down to bed rock. Why did you give him the money?

## ASSURANCE

Of course, you'll be all right. The doctor said you were ever so much better.

Don't worry! You're safe. The stock is good as gold.

## AUTHORITY

I don't want any *ifs* or *ands* or *buts* or *whys* about it. It will be done just as I order.

Dismiss her. I don't want her services any longer.

## BOASTING

Work? Huh! He ought to be in my shoes for a day! I do more in a week than he does in a year.

Say, it was a cinch. When you want results, just get your Uncle Dudley on the job.

## CONFIDENCE

There is no question about it. I have confidence—absolute confidence in him.

Man, we're bound to win. They don't stand a ghost of a chance.

## CONFUSION

Well—I intended—but—you wouldn't understand—of course....

Hardly, but still—oh, I suppose—well, honestly I don't know what to say about it.

## CONTEMPT

Huh! I wouldn't drag myself down to his level.

I'll just ignore him. Ignorant. He doesn't know any better. I pity him. Honestly, I do.

## CONVICTION

You *think*, but I *know*. See?

He's dead right. I know it. You wouldn't change my mind in a thousand years.

## COURAGE

Well, it is right; and I am going to see it through no matter what it costs.

It isn't a question of being afraid. I'll face anyone.

## DISPRAISE

She is a miserable stenographer. Doesn't know how to punctuate or spell. Sloppy and careless!

Don't make me laugh. An M.D.? Huh! He wouldn't make a first-class horse doctor.

## DISAPPOINTMENT

I expected more of him. That's a great disappointment.

Everything has gone wrong this winter. Every single man I've hired has had to be fired. Not a dollar profit this month. Believe me, it takes the heart out of a man.

## ENCOURAGEMENT

Great! Now, that's what I call progress. Keep right on, my boy, keep right on.

Don't give up. Persistence, that's what you need—keep everlastingly at it. Of course, you can't make a sale every week. We don't expect you to. But, keep on. We're satisfied. You ought to be.

## IMPATIENCE

Please, don't interrupt me. You annoy me to death.

For Heaven's sake, be quiet. I am tired and nervous. I'm in no mood for foolishness.

## INDIFFERENCE

Do as you please. I don't care.

Oh—anything you say.

## IRONY

Oh, sure, you are interested—very—anybody could see that.

He is an expert—a genius—especially in his own estimation.

## MODESTY

Don't mention it. It was nothing. Anybody would have done the same.

You are very kind, but really you exaggerate. I'm a very ordinary person.

## PERPLEXITY

Let me see. I thought he wrote me to come today. It might have been yesterday! I've forgotten.

Go three blocks west, or four, and then turn—to the right, I think. I'm not positive about that. You had better ask someone else.

## PITY

Poor girl! I certainly feel sorry for her.

What a pity! What a pity!

## REFUSAL

I can't grant your request. I'm sorry, but I

can't.

Impossible! I refuse positively. I won't have a thing to do with it.

## RESIGNATION

Oh, well, it can't be helped. We may as well grin and bear it.

What's the use? If it can't be changed, it can't, that's all.

## SECRECY

Shh! Keep this under your hat.

Just between you and me and the gate post, I am not going to let out a peep about this matter.

## STUBBORNNESS

You couldn't change my mind in a thousand years.

You can say all you want to, but I know what I'm talking about. I won't budge an inch.

## THREAT

Just try it if you dare. I'll get even with you.

If he puts that order through, I'll make it hot for him.

## URGING

See this thing through at once. It's important.

You can do it and we expect you to do it. Go on, don't give up now. Don't.

### WELCOME
Come right in. I'm mighty glad to see you.
Sure, you're welcome as the flowers in May.

## 84. Ways of Developing Expression

The secret of good delivery is enlarged naturalness. Truly, but what is the secret of enlarged naturalness? In other words, what are the things we do in conversation that we leave undone in public address? If you analyze natural, unaffected conversation, you will discover five very important things that are often lacking in public address.

We shall discuss them in the order given here:

1. Speaking forcefully the words that carry the main ideas and hurrying the words that stand for the important ideas.

2. Changing the rate of speaking.

3. Pausing before or after important thoughts.

4. Changing the pitch of the voice.

5. Giving color to the tones.

## 85. Changing the Force and Rate of Speaking

Listen to people converse. You will notice that they continually change their rate of speaking. They may vary all the way from thirty to two hundred and fifty words a minute in the same conversation.

Important, dignified, and intense thoughts usually require slow movement. Trivial and subordinated thoughts are spoken faster.

By changing the speed of expression, speakers can impart strength and importance or lightness and insignificance to their statements.

For example, say "thirty million dollars," quickly and superficially, so it will sound like thirty cents. Repeat it, give each syllable in a slow, earnest tone; note the impressiveness of the result.

Read aloud the following. Go slowly over the words in bold italics. Hurry over the others. Notice how this makes your main points stand out boldly:

"***Selling goods*** is a ***battle*** and ***only fighters*** can ***win*** out in it. We may not like these conditions, but we didn't have the making of them, and we ***can't alter*** them…. ***Take your courage*** with you when you enter the selling game. If you don't ***you'll strike out*** every time you come to bat, and score nothing higher than a string of goose eggs. ***No man*** ever made a ***three base hit*** who was ***afraid*** of the ***pitcher***—remember that. The fellow who knocks the cover off the ball, or lifts it over the fence for a home run, is always the chap who steps up to the plate with **grim determination** in his heart." — From an address to salesmen in "Ginger Talks," by W. C. Holman.

Too many speeches are like a phonograph French lesson; they pound right ahead from beginning to end as if the speaker were doing the quarter-mile run.

## 86. Pausing Before or After Important Thoughts

An advertising firm which pays $5,000 for a page advertisement doesn't print it full of words. The Ad. men know that white paper brings out the sense of the message on the page. Conversation, too, is full of white space, *pauses—holes*. The public addresses of the best speakers are also like that.

The conversations you hear and overhear and full of pauses. Observe the technique of good speakers and actors. They stop suddenly before a significant word; after a moment of silence, they hurl the word across like the bark of a pistol. A pause forces attention on the words following it.

The National Cash Register people tell their salesmen:

"Pause before you make an important point. It excites the prospect's interest. It arouses his curiosity. When you have made your point, give it time to soak in."

In the following excerpt from "Ginger Talks," I have marked the places where a speaker might profitably pause.

Read this aloud without pausing. Then read it again, pausing for a second where I have indicated. Note the effect of these pauses:

"Selling goods is a battle (pause and let the idea of *battle* soak in) and only fighters can win in it. (Pause and let that point soak in.) We may not like these conditions (pause and hold your hearer in suspense as to what is coming next) but we didn't have the making of them (pause) and we can't alter them (pause).... Take your courage with you when you enter the selling game (pause). If you don't (pause and lengthen out suspense for a second) you'll strike out every time you come to bat, and score nothing higher than a string of goose eggs (pause). No man ever made a three base hit (pause for suspense) who was afraid of the pitcher (pause and let your point soak in)—remember that. (Pause and let it soak in some more.) The fellow who knocks the cover off the ball, or lifts it over the fence for a home run (pause and increase the suspense as to what you are going to say about this marvelous player) is always the chap who steps up to the plate with grim determination in his heart."

~ ~ ~

Read the following and make pauses where you think they ought to be.

"Always remember that when you are talking to a prospective customer you are like a man walking about in a dynamite factory—the slightest misstep is likely to blow you out through the roof, so far as any chance of landing a sale is concerned. You customer isn't a bag of sand or a load of rock. He is a man—made up of combustibles—pride, prejudices, vanity, sensitiveness, conceit. Be careful not to touch a match to any of these; avoid friction—it throws out sparks. Walk gently—make your advances with caution, as a man feels his way in the dark. And at every stage of the proceedings remember that a spoonful of smile is worth a gallon of growl." —From an address to salesmen, in "Ginger Talks," by W. C. Holman.

## 87. Changing the Pitch of the Voice

Listen to yourself or anyone else converse, and notice that there is a continual change in the pitch of the voice. It is always shifting from lower to higher pitches and vice versa.

In conversation this tone change is very common.

In public address it is—I regret to say—very rare.

You have heard public speakers, haven't you, who spoke in one pitch—usually a high one—until your ears almost hurt? *Continually speaking in one monotonous pitch is one of the worst faults of delivery.*

If you are speaking on a low pitch and want to make a word or groups of words stand out boldly, throw them into a high pitch or vice versa. The main thing is to speak in a *different* pitch.

Speak the following sentences aloud. Put the bold italicized words in a high pitch, the other in a low pitch or vice versa. Note the results.

"***We find in life*** exactly what we put in it."

— Emerson

"***I will listen to anyone's convictions***, but pray keep your doubts to yourself." — Goethe


## 88. Giving Color to the Tones

What do I mean by tone color?

Let me illustrate. Can't you recall the metallic, monotonous tones that an elevator operator in a department store uses when calling out: "Fifth floor, carpets, rugs, furniture, musical instruments, pianos"?

Can you recall the raspingly high, machine-like and lifeless tones that you have heard some speakers use—especially speakers delivering memorized words?

Don't those tones, now that you think of them, appear to be pale and without color and warmth?

Warm and colorful tones? You have heard yourself use them thousands of times when you were intensely in earnest and conscious only of what you were saying. You almost always have warm, colorful tones when you are speaking with feeling—anger or joy, love or hate.

If you can step on the magic carpet of memory and transport yourself back to the roseate day in the long ago when you took the most wonderful woman in the world in your arms and told her of your love—if you can only hear yourself speaking those words again, you will have the most vivid illustration of tone color and warmth.

Pale, gray, monotonous tones seem to be the rule and not the exception in public address.

*Strive for the warm, colorful tones—tones that are pleasing to the ear and expressive. There is nothing in delivery so important.*

## 89. Essentials of Good Delivery

We have practically all the essentials of delivery when we are speaking with abandon and feeling in ordinary conversation.

We must reproduce on the platform the same conditions that produce these qualities in conversation. In other words, we must speak before an audience with feeling, spontaneity, abandon, and enlarged naturalness.

Students don't need drilling in the technique of delivery or the various kinds of tones or gestures so much as they need to let themselves go, to relax, to speak with earnestness and freedom and feeling.

If you feel that your delivery is stiff and stilted and not getting across, just pause a moment and say to yourself silently, "I didn't come here to hurl a speech at these people. I came here to talk to them—as one human being talks to another."

Don't merely *say* that. *Do* it. Pick out one individual in your audience and talk to him. Forget everyone else for the time being and *talk* to him.

Crowds don't want to hear so-called orators hurl memorized speeches into the air. Crowds don't want to be talked at, they want to be talked to. So speak like a human being, not like an automaton—and people will hear you gladly.

Ten

# *The Attractive Speech*

## 90. The Attractive Speech

"Nothing else will call out what is in a man so quickly and so effectively as the constant effort to do his best in speaking before an audience. When one undertakes to think on his feet and speak extemporaneously before the public, the power and the skill of the entire man are put to a severe test.

"The practice of public speaking, the effort to marshal all one's forces in a logical and forceful manner, to bring to a focus all the power one possesses, is a great awakener of all the faculties. The sense of power that comes from holding the attention, stirring the emotions, or convincing the reason of an audience, gives self-confidence, assurance, self-reliance, arouses ambition and tends to make one more effective in every way.

"One's judgment, education, manhood, character, all the things that go to make a man what he is, are being unrolled like a panorama in his effort to express himself. Every mental faculty is quickened, every power of thought and expression stirred and spurred."

— Dr. Orison Swett Marden

## 91. *Setting the Stage for Speaking*

Guests on the platform won't sit absolutely still; if possible, therefore, *do not permit others to occupy a seat on the platform while you are speaking.*

I remember trying to listen to Raymond Robins when his platform was crowded with guests of honor. Every time they moved the slightest bit, the entire audience looked at them and away from the speaker.

In the play "On Trial" an attorney addressed a stage jury, but they had been trained not to move a muscle. The stage director knew that if the members of his jury moved a little, even unconsciously, they would kill the effect of the attorney's speech.

Actors know the effect of moving while someone is speaking and if one Thespian is angry with another, he moves during the other fellow's big lines to kill their effect.

~ ~ ~

It is not advisable to speak from a platform cluttered up with furniture, and maps, and signs. These things give an impression of confusion and distract your hearers' attention.

~ ~ ~

Don't stand behind tables or chairs. Have you noticed people in the end seats who were leaning out in the aisle so that they could look at *all* of the speaker?

One of the best known political speakers in this country is ex-Governor Leslie M. Shaw. On one occasion, I introduced him to an audience from a platform with a speaker's table in the center. He immediately walked to the table, grasped it in both hands and carried it off the stage. He knew it was wise to stand so that his hearers could see him from head to foot.

Haven't you often hear it said of someone that "he likes the center of the stage"? That is an expression borrowed, of course, from stage parlance. The stage director knows that *whatever holds the center of the stage, dominates the stage*. Where you are speaking don't let a piece of furniture dominate and weaken you.

Try this out for yourself. Stage a little scene in front of a mirror. Place a large chair or table in front of you and begin to speak. Now remove the furniture and speak with nothing to obstruct your view. This little experiment will drive the point home more efficaciously than will a half dozen more paragraphs of print.

## 92. *Use of Platform*

When addressing a large audience, you will find that a platform will help you to be seen and heard. It also tends to give you a position of authority.

The president of one of New York's largest banks has his desk on a shallow platform. This shrewd psychologist realizes that compelling his visitors to look up to him physically tends to produce a corresponding mental attitude. Another executive, for the same reason, insists that those interviewing him sit while he stands.

However, if you are talking to a small group, a high platform is too formal. If you stand down on a level with, and close to your hearers, you can get a much more intimate touch.

## 93. *Approaching the Platform*

You reveal yourself as you walk out before an audience. The moment that you make your entrance your audience unconsciously feels whether or not you are in earnest.

Imitate the walk of the man you desire to be. Walk and stand like a man of action and enthusiasm.

I have seen speakers nullify by their lacka-

daisical manner of standing, every strong statement that they made.

The manner in which you come before an
audience is an important detail. You have doubtless
seen speakers arrive from their chairs and amble to
the front of the platform as lackadaisically as a
superannuated army mule. You have also seen and
*felt* men swing out before their hearers with the
busy, animated air of a curb-broker during rush
hours; by their very movements they impressed you
with the fact that they were worth listening to.
Their spirited steps and energetic presence commanded attention. Put into your entrance some of
the snap of a bayonet drill.


## 94. On the Platform

Don't be in a hurry after you appear before
your audience. Haste at that moment indicates
nervousness and a lack of self-control. Take your
time; the audience will wait.

The average speaker begins too soon and
then speaks too slowly.

Look occasionally from one part of the audience to another giving each individual the impression that you are directing your remarks to him.

And don't forget the friends in the rear rows;
they need attention in their turn.

## 95. Leaving the Platform

When you finish, don't turn your back to the audience and walk off with the hauteur of a top sergeant leading a platoon of rookies. Show your respect by stepping backward a little toward the side of the platform opposite your seat, and then walk obliquely to your chair.

## 96. Technique of Sitting Down and Rising

A stage director severely reprimanded an actor who was playing the role of a gentleman for sitting down in the conventional way: he looked around to be sure that he was close to the chair, doubled up, and awkwardly flopped down.

A man of refinement feeling the seat strike the back of his leg will not be compelled to turn around and look with the modified movements of a dog preparing to lie down. His back from the hips to head remains easily erect, and his body under perfect controls sinks into his chair.

Now stand before a mirror and try out these two methods for yourself, and see which strikes you as being the more refined.

You can determine the degree of a speaker's earnestness by the manner in which he sits down or gets up out of his seat.

You audience may not stop to analyze these things, but if you get up in a lazy I-don't-care manner your hearers won't be impressed, no matter what you say.

When you sit down, keep perfect control of yourself. Don't flop down. Sink into your seat easily. Thus you will suggest self-control and power. You will win confidence.

When you get up out of your seat, arise like a man who is keenly alive and knows what he is about.

Study for a fortnight the way people rise and notice how it affects you.

## 97. Power of First Impressions

Every time a person meets you, he sizes you up swiftly.

It takes him about as long to score you as it does a champion trap shooter to break a clay pigeon. These instantaneous ratings, you are getting all the time, have much to do with your prosperity and happiness.

*Do you realize that these rapid estimates are usually based on three things—what you say, how you say it, and the way you look, dress, and bear yourself?*

If a man looks sleepy and anemic and stands

and walks listlessly, people will believe his looks and not waste time on him. If his trousers are baggy, his hair unkempt, and his shoes dingy—they will pay him as little respect as he pays himself. But if he is vigorous and alert in his bearing, and takes pride in his clothes and personal appearance, he will usually radiate success and command attention.

Being well groomed is a towering asset to a speaker either in a business interview or on the platform. John L. Shuff, who has written more insurance than any other man in the United States, said:

"When I started in the insurance business twenty years ago, I realized that to make a good appearance was to look prosperous, and I paid much attention to my dress.

"If you have only one suit of clothes, keep that one suit clean and pressed all the time. Press your trousers yourself every day, if necessary. And keep your shoes shined."

## 98. Your Appearance Influences Your Own Morale

Your personal appearance not only impresses other people; it also has a big influence on your own morale.

Dr. G. Stanley Hall sent a series of questions

on the psychology of dress to one hundred and seventy young people.

"All of them testified that when they looked successful they found it easy to feel and act successful. When they felt shabby their ability to deal successfully with other men and women took a decided drop.

"When they were poorly dressed, they shrank from facing other people; they felt themselves at a disadvantage; they instinctively met other men on terms of inequality when they ought to have met them on terms of equality."

The Italians say: "Respect yourself as the first step to the respect of others." *The consciousness of being well dressed largely increases one's self-esteem.*

A New York philanthropic institution gave the human unfortunates drifting about the Bowery not only religious teaching but new heels. These derelicts were both figuratively and literally "down at the heels." A cobbler was hired to repair the worn shoes of those who shuffled across the threshold—*because it had been noticed that a man whose heels were mended, stood straighter physically and morally, possessed increased self-respect, and exerted more will-power.*

A big business man failed suddenly. The newspapers headlined the fact that he had drawn from his personal bank account his last dollar to buy a suit of clothes. He had realized that attractive wearing apparel would help to restore his courage and make easier the rehabilitation of his business.

## 99. *How to Ruin the Effect of Expensive Apparel*

Many men have ruined the effect of expensive wearing apparel by carrying a can of Velvet Joe, the evening paper, a flashlight, meerschaum pipe, and similar valuables in their coat pockets! Furthermore, the man who is careful of his attire never has a Waterman or a yellow pencil peeping out of his upper left-hand pocket, neither is he bedecked with buttons or badges.

## 100. *Control Yourself Physically*

*If you want to impress people as a man of dignity and poise, control yourself physically.*

You instinctively feel that the man who controls himself is mightier than he that taketh a city; and you also feel that the man who fidgets about in his chair, shifts from foot to foot, or doesn't know what to do with his hands, does not control himself.

Speakers sometimes fall into nervous mannerisms which divert attention from their addresses. Even Dr. Frank Crane, the noted apostle of common sense, when speaking, played with a scarf on a table in front of him and pulled the attention of the audience away from his message to his moving finger.

There is a New York man, extraordinarily successful in business, who, when he attempts to make a public address, gives his hands a dry wash, buttons and unbuttons his coat, and does a sort of sublimated fox-trot back and forth across the platform.

All right, now let us start at once applying this secret power which we have just been discussing.

When you talk in the office, on the street, or before an audience, keep control of yourself physically. *Remember that every movement that does not add to, detracts.*

Don't be stiff and stilted; make all the movements necessary and advisable, *but beware of unnecessary ones.*

## 101. Technique of Gestures

I have drilled legions of students who neglected to gesture when speaking in public. Many of them declared that gestures didn't come naturally to them and that they never gestured in conversation. However, I discovered that by drawing these same students into a controversy regarding some phase of their speeches or their habits, they would soon be gesturing unconsciously in the conversation with me.

Almost everyone uses actions to help express himself in everyday talk. Truly, *"Actions speak plainer than words."* It is altogether surprising how much one can express by actions and gestures alone—without the aid of words.

After years of experimenting, I have found it imperative to insist that student speakers use gestures. Singular as it may seem to some, this is done not so much because of the effect that it will have on the audience as because of the effect it will have on the speaker himself.

The moment you begin to use gestures you will begin to speak with a new abandon. You will let yourself go and speak naturally. More color will creep into your voice, more earnestness and more soul.

I have delivered hundreds of travel lectures in connection with colored slides and motion pictures. Naturally, in such circumstances, my auditors were looking at the screen, not at me. I stood in the dark, but I always gestured as if I were in the glare of the footlights. I knew the audience would not see my gestures, but I knew also that the audience would feel them through the tones of my voice.

Watch yourself today, especially when you speak vigorously, and notice the simple gestures you make.

They help you to make yourself understood and forceful, but somehow no one is conscious that you are making them.

*Whenever you see a gesture as a gesture, it is bad; it has defeated its very reason for existence—it has taken away from your thought, not helped it.*

## 102. Psychology of Gestures

You gesture fairly well in private.

The next time you speak before an audience, let yourself go when you feel an impulse to gesture, just as you do in conversation, and you will have solved half the problem of gesturing.

You may not be able to gesture naturally at first; when you first use your hands on the platform, you may feel as if something had broken loose inside you and you may expect people to laugh, but they won't. Gesture, no matter how awkward it feels, and you will improve as you practice—you can rest assured of that.

## 103. Practice Gestures

No one could give you a hand-me-down set of gestures. Gestures, like wives, depend largely on the man; what is proper for one won't suit the personality of another. However, *just for the sake of practice*, I want you try, as you say the accompanying sentences, the gestures I have set down here:

1. "I ask of you in all fairness, am I getting a square deal?"

As you say that, hold your hands out in front of you with palms up—just as you might naturally do in asking a question.

2. "It's a lie! And he doesn't dare deny it!"

Close all of your hand except your forefinger; shake it vigorously as you hurl out this indictment.

3. "No. No. I wouldn't do that."

Hold your hand out with the back of it facing you—the movement that a policeman uses to hold up traffic.

4. "He tossed the whole matter aside, and refused to have anything to do with it."

Use about the movement that you would employ to toss something to one side.

5. "He has made a  mistake, of course, but let's keep quiet about it."

Extend your hand in front of you, palm downward, as if you were pushing something down.


Watch your gestures. Do you use a variety? Or do you use one or two pet ones for everything?

You are urged to enlarge your repertoire of actions; to acquire the fine points of gesturing.

Study people. Watch them gesture. Imitate the gestures that strike you as forceful.

Observe that the foundation of good gesture is suggestion.

If you are trying to sneak up on a flock of wild ducks and your companion or your dog rises to look over the bank, what kind of gesture would you naturally use to make him sit down again?

Wouldn't you use a similar gesture if you said, "We must keep this deal under cover"?

Wouldn't the gesture in both instances suggest secrecy?

When do  you gesture with a clenched fist in conversation? Why not use a clenched fist when expressing similar ideas on a public platform?

What gestures do people use in an appeal or a welcome? Watch yourself and others. See which kind of gesture is used unconsciously in conversation. Use these gestures in public speaking.

When would you use a wide sweep of the hand in gesturing?

When do people use the extended index finger? What suggestion does it give? Watch and see.

*Don't ask for an iron-clad set of rules for gesturing. Use your eyes—and your common sense.*

## 104. Facial Expression

William Jennings Bryan said that he wore neither a mustache nor a beard in order that he might have the full value of his facial expression in speaking.

Did you ever notice how much of a conversation or an address depends upon the facial expression of the speaker? Have you tried to listen to a speaker whom you could not see? If so, you realize that you were getting only about half his speech.

## 105. Natural Facial Expression

The probabilities are that you have fairly adequate facial expression when you are speaking naturally to a few friends—especially if you are speaking under the influence of some emotion such as anger, love, jealousy, excitement, hate.

If you would only use as much facial expression before an audience as you do in conversation, we might possibly be satisfied. But you don't, so you ought deliberately to train yourself to employ your natural facial expression while speaking until you use it unconsciously.

## 106. Enlarge Your Natural Facial Expression

In facial expression just as in delivery our shibboleth is *enlarged naturalness.*

When addressing an audience, you must exaggerate slightly your facial expressions as well as your tones.

## 107. Practice Facial Expressions

Practice before your mirror a few particularly telling facial expressions.

Of course, I recognize that you are a business or a professional man and that you have no ambitions to become a second Booth or to compete with Douglas Fairbanks for screen honors. You know and I know that if you were to get up in a business conference and use the exaggerated facial expressions that one often sees in the movies, your business associates would laugh at you.

I am not advocating any such course of action: nevertheless it will be profitable for you to study facial expression just as an actor might do. If you will, in the privacy of your own room and before your cheval glass, try to reproduce some of the facial expressions that you observe in art galleries, on the street, and in the movies, the practice will have a salutary effect.

If this practice did nothing else than teach you the value of facial expression and of limbering up your facial muscles, it would be paying its freight, wouldn't it?

## 108. Smile Often

*I know of nothing else that will win the heart and confidence of an audience so readily as a smile.*

It is generally conceded that "nothing succeeds like success." Well, few things bespeak success and contentment more quickly than a smile. A man's smile seems to say: "Things go pretty much as I desire. I have found the world an excellent place to live in. I meet with success everywhere."

You like such a person as that; you unconsciously have confidence in him.

*The value of a smile in speaking is almost incalculable.* Some years ago I was writing an article for *The American Magazine* about a certain bank president in New York. I asked one of his associates the reason for this man's success. No small amount of it, he replied, was attributable to the man's smile.

You realize that a smile can be cultivated.

You realize also that it wins dollars and friends and smiles in return.

## 109. Developing Correct Carriage

As you walk along the street tomorrow try to judge people from their manner of standing and walking. After you have formed you estimate of them by observing their walk and pose, look at their faces and general get-up and see how accurate your judgment is.

Notice how age moves and stands, and youth, and physical brawn, and the laggard, and the man of action. Each one of them discloses himself in his walk.

Look at the heels of your shoes; if they are worn off more behind than in front, you don't walk correctly. That shows that your heels strike the floor first. If you walk correctly, your heels and the balls of your feet would strike the floor at the same instant.

*Walk with your weight on the balls of your feet, and your chest will be higher, your head more erect, your abdomen back where it belongs, and you will have a better personal appearance. Try it and see.*

When you stand correctly, your heels act merely as a balance, not as a support for your weight.

Here is a test to show you whether you stand with your weight on the balls of your feet. Stand up—right now. Place your heels together, hands on your hips. Now rise slowly on your toes. Do you have to sway your body forward a little way before you rise?

If so, you are out of poise just so much.

Now, standing just as you naturally do, try it again.

A good exercise to develop correct placement of your weight is to walk about the room for several minutes with the heels free of the floor and the weight, of course, entirely on the toes.

*Hold your chest high, so that it would strike first if you strode against the wall.*

Does you chest strike first? Walk against the wall now and see.

## 110. Developing Will Power

*Daily exercise will tone up your system and give you command of yourself.*

If a man is nervous and run down physically, he doesn't give an impression of power when he faces a business man in his office or an audience from a platform.

"Man must first of all be a good animal."

One of the most important of your concerns is your physical fitness.

Unless you are one man in a score, you are clipping from five to ten years off your life by neglecting to take the proper amount of physical exercise.

I am going to give you some of the setting-up exercises used in the army. Force yourself—and believe me, you won't do it unless you do force yourself—to go through these exercises before an open window for ten minutes each morning; and you will have more poise, and smartness, and precision, do your work better and with less fatigue, relish your food more, get more refreshment from sleep, and add years to your life.

*One of the biggest things you will gain from this daily drill is will power. Four-fifths of public speaking is sheer will, that is, the power of self-direction.*

And after you have tried getting up every

morning for a month to exercise, you will agree with me that there are few things beneath the Southern Cross or the North Star that demand more will power in their execution.

~ ~ ~

The army drills our boys in khaki to stand in the position of attention, "which is a position of coordination, of physical and mental alertness, which makes for mobility, activity, and grace." Here it is:

1. *Heels together and on a line.*
2. *Feet turned out equally, forming an angle of forty-five degrees.*
3. *Knees extended without stiffness*, muscles contracted just enough to keep knees straight.
4. *Trunk erect upon hips.* You should feel your trunk stretch up from the waist until the back is practically straight.
5. *Shoulders falling naturally* and moved back until they are square.
6. *Arms hanging naturally*, palms toward you and fingers relaxed.
7. *Head erect, chin raised* until neck is vertical, eyes fixed on some object at their own level.

Get up now and practice standing at attention. Watch your method of walking and standing until you develop the much-prized military carriage. It will pay you socially and financially.

~ ~ ~

Start these exercises from the position of "attention." Repeat each exercise ten times. Between each exercise touch the palms of your hands together three times high above your head; inhale deeply as you raise your arms; exhale as you drop them.

### ONE
Hands on hips: (1) Bend trunk forward until it is at right angles to the legs—hips perpendicular—exhale; (2) raise trunk to upright position and inhale.

### TWO
Hands on hips: (1) Rise on toes, smartly; (2) lower heels gently.

### THREE
Hands on hips: Bend head forward and backward, stretching the neck muscles.

### FOUR
Hands on shoulders: (1) Twist trunk side-

ward, right, inhale; (2) same left, exhale.

## FIVE

Hands on hips: Bend trunk sideward to the right as far as possible, stretching the waist muscles, inhale; (2) same left, exhale.

## SIX

Hands on hips: Raise knees forward alternately until they are on a line level with the hips.

Eleven

# *The Distinctive Speech*

## 111. The Distinctive Speech

*"We should be as careful of words as of our actions."* — Cicero

*"I hold it as a great point in self-education, that the student be continually engaged in forming exact ideas, and in expressing them clearly by language."* — Faraday

*"It should be a matter of conscience not to misuse words; it should also be a matter of conscience to resist the misuse of them."*
— Herbert Spencer

*"I hope you will from the start cultivate public speaking. The power of speaking with grace and energy, the power of using aright the best words of our noble language, is itself a fortune and a reputation if it is associated and enriched by knowledge and sense."* — Rufus Choate, in a letter written to his son in Amherst College

## 112. *Your Choice of Words*

Your education and culture are reflected by your language.

Your words advertise you!

Do you know the difference between a venturesome, a chivalrous, a daring, a dauntless, a doughty, a fearless, an intrepid, a courageous, a valiant, a heroic, and a bold man? Or would you characterize him as brave and let it go at that?

Your words advertise you.

I recently heard a conversation between two women that sounded like this:

"Wouldn't it be awful nice if Nellie could go too?"

"Yeh, just perfectly grand."

"I feel awful sorry for her."

"Isn't it perfectly awful the way he treats her?"

I didn't need to listen to any more to know that their mental equipment was rusty.

## 113. *Your Language is a Barometer of Your Mental Condition*

Two of the most eminent educators of this generation have gone on record as saying that your language is a barometer of your mental condition:

Nicholas Murray Butler, President of Columbia University, said:

"Correctness and precision in the use of the mother tongue is one of the first marks of an educated man."

And Charles W. Eliot, President Emeritus of Harvard University, has declared:

"I recognize but one mental acquisition as a necessary part of the education of a lady or gentleman, namely, an accurate and refined use of the mother tongue."

Woodrow Wilson is superbly skillful with the English language. Here is his own story of how he learned to marshal words:

"My father never allowed any member of his household to use an incorrect expression. Any slip on the part of one of the children was at once corrected; any unfamiliar word was immediately explained; each of us was encouraged to find a use for it in our conversation so as to fix it in our memories."

*Go thou and do likewise! Look up in an unabridged dictionary all unfamiliar words you encounter. (If you don't own a large dictionary, you should invest in one at once.)*

## 114. Words in Everyday Conversation

We are now going to obey this dictum of the elder Wilson. You know the meaning of the following words, don't you? If you don't look them up.

*And this is important too: Find uses for them in your conversation soon so as to fix them in your memory. They may seem strange at first; but employ a word five times and it is yours.*

| | | |
|---|---|---|
| inadequate | sedulous | conversant |
| remiss | vivacious | garrulous |
| recalcitrant | inimitable | enigma |
| equanimity | deter | meticulous |
| versatile | animosity | facetious |
| magnanimous | tacit | precarious |
| dubious | agile | incontestable |

When you have made these words your own, assimilate another group, and you will be on the high road toward developing distinction in diction.

## 115. Slang

A little slang now and then is used by the best of men: President Wilson spoke of men "talking through their hats." The trouble with slang is that most people overwork it. It stunts their language. Too much of it bespeaks a sparsely furnished mind. We all know men who are mentally too lazy and incompetent to choose exact words. I never knew them to speak of anything as delightful, delicious, handsome, charming, elegant, exquisite, picturesque, rare, extraordinary, amazing, remarkable, singular, unique, splendid, magnificent, or superb.

Anything that ought to be described by such terms is, in their argot, "cool."

Pause right now and write down some of the slang terms that you work overtime. Resolve to avoid them in the future.

## 116. *Phrases to Avoid*

Here is a bevy of phrases which were superannuated a hundred years before Rip Van Winkle dozed off into his celebrated slumber. Threadbare and hackneyed, they are offensive to most educated people. To use them is to advertise that you are mentally careless. If you are guilty of using any of the phrases in the following list, put an X opposite your weaknesses and resolve to shun them:

I come before you unprepared.

Never to be forgotten.

Yours of the 16th inst. at hand.

In reply we beg to say.

We view with alarm.
I shall not inflict a speech on you.
As the hour is growing late.
One word more and I have done.
I might talk to you for hours.
I have already taken up too much time.
Leave no stone unturned.
Cheered to the echo.
Haled into court.
The irony of fate.
I am no orator.
We point with pride.
From pillar to post.
The more, the merrier.
Wend their way.
Abreast of the times.
As luck would have it.
Monarch of all I survey.
All work and no play, etc.
The staff of life.
Bold as a lion.
Lords of creation.
Throw cold water upon.
To curry favor.
Beck and call.
To and fro.
With might and main.

## 117. How to Study Words

How ample a stock of words do you have to draw from? Milton used eight thousand, Shakespeare fifteen thousand. The Standard Dictionary contains half a million. But the average man bungles along on half a thousand or so. Mentally he is slothful, and when he speaks, you know his brain isn't functioning.

Kipling spent hours at a time studying the dictionary—and his writing shows it.

The only reason you don't talk better is—yourself. You are not willing to force yourself to study, to practice with words as you would practice for a tennis match.

## 118. Practice Rewriting

Benjamin Franklin used to rewrite pages of some English classic. He would then compare his efforts with the original, and discover his weaknesses. Try a similar exercise: Write in your own words this famous letter from Lincoln to Mrs. Bixby:

"Dear Madam: I have been shown, in the files of the War Department, a statement of the Adjutant-General of Massachusetts, that you are the mother of five sons who have died gloriously on the field of battle. I feel how weak and fruitless must be any words of mine which should attempt to beguile you from a loss so overwhelming. But I cannot refrain from tendering to you the consolation that may be found in the thanks of the Republic they died to save. I pray that our Heavenly Father may assuage the anguish of your bereavement, and leave you only the cherished memory of the loved and lost and the solemn pride that must be yours to have laid so costly a sacrifice upon the alter of freedom.

    Yours very sincerely and respectfully,
                    Abraham Lincoln."

~ ~ ~

Rewrite the leading editorial in your newspaper tomorrow. Like all newspaper material, it is written hastily; perhaps you can, with a little care, improve it.

Make this experiment with some of the articles appearing in your favorite magazines.

*119. Read Aloud*

Read aloud some of Stevenson's essays or novels. You will have a good time doing it, and it will replenish your exchequer of words. Study

Stevenson's words. Get the feel of phrases. Sensitize your ear to niceties of diction.

Read aloud this bit from Stevenson's "Virginibus Puerisque":

"Marriage is terrifying, but so is a cold and forlorn old age. The friendships of men are vastly agreeable, but they are insecure. You know all the time that one friend will marry and put you to the door; a second accept a situation in China, and become no more to you than a name, a reminiscence, and an occasional crossed letter, very laborious to read; a third will take up with some religious crotchet and treat you to sour looks thenceforward. So, in one way or another, life forces men apart and breaks up the goodly fellowships forever. The very flexibility and ease which make men's friendships so agreeable while they endure, make them easier to destroy and forget. And a man who has a few friends, or one who has a dozen (if there be anyone so wealthy on this earth), cannot forget on how precarious a base his happiness reposes."

~ ~ ~

People who go in for collecting large words are apt to use them unsuitably. Having a character misuse words is one of the oldest comic tricks on the stage. You remember that Mrs. Malaprop said, "I've been declining on the sofa, pursuing the dictionary."

*Skilled writers and speakers use few strange words. They employ words which you understand but don't use.*

## 120. How to Use Comparisons

Discriminating writers, conversationalists, and speakers refrain from much-used expressions. For example, no man with a vestige of originality in speaking of a thing being cold would make the ice, or cucumber, comparison. For example, here are some of the similes that have been used by careful writers to express cold:

Cold as a dog's nose.

Cold as a frog.

Cold as a hot-water bag in the morning.

Cold as a tomb.

Cold as iron.

Cold as the heart of a courtesan.

Cold as clay. — Coleridge

Cold as a turtle. — Richard Cumberland

Cauld as the drifting snow. — Allan Cunningham

Cold as salt. — James Huneker

Cold as an earthworm. — Maurice Maeterlinck

Cold as dawn.

Cold as rain in autumn.

~ ~ ~

Think up some similes of your own to convey the idea of coldness, and write them now. Don't put down something you have heard. Take enough time to think of some new things that are cold. *Have the courage to be distinctive.*

Never sacrifice the picturesque and effective employment of words to custom and rut-worn usage. Say whatever words will most beautifully and forcefully carry your meaning, regardless of whether anyone has ever ventured to use the same combination of words previously.

Write your similes here:

Cold as _____.

Cold as _____.

Cold as _____.

Cold as _____.

Cold as _____.

Don't let your originality in phrasing perish with the creation of these few similes. Carry it on into your daily conversation and public addresses.

Precision and originality in language usually lead to precision and originality in thought.

## 121. Use of Synonyms

As you read the following list of words, place in the margin an X beside those groups with whose distinction you are already familiar. Place an O alongside the other groups.

Don't attempt to digest all of this at once. After reading the list, go back to the beginning and fix in your mind, so that you will never forget it, the exact distinction within one group of words. Write in the margin the date on which you mastered these words. Tomorrow night assimilate another group, and write the date in the margin. This is what will count—a little effort each day: not an hour's study now and negligence ever after.

Place this book in your bedroom where it will catch your eye just before you retire. Only a minute will be required to perform your daily stunt. This little bit each day, will, as time goes on, bring surprising expertness.

This practice has richly repaid others. It will repay you a thousand fold for all the time and energy expended. Try it and see.

**Amass—Accumulate**. (Wrong) "He spent his entire life *amassing* his wealth." *Accumulate* expresses a gradual, *amass* a rapid, gathering.

**Anticipate—Expect**. *Anticipate* means more than merely *expect*; it suggests forecasting, taking measures to meet. If you *expect* a storm you may *anticipate* it by taking your raincoat.

**Antipathy—Dislike**. *Antipathy* is instinctive; *dislike* is often acquired. You have an *antipathy* for criminals; you may *dislike* your landlord.

**Authentic—Genuine**. *Authentic* suggests possessing authority and being true to the facts; *genuine* means, not counterfeit. If a Sandwich Islander wrote a book on ice hockey and signed his name to it, the treatise would be *genuine* but probably not *authentic*.

**Behavior—Conduct**. *Behavior* refers to our mode of acting in the presence of others—it generally refers to a specific instance. *Conduct* refers to the general tone of our actions in the more serious aspects of life.

**But—And**. "Poor *but* honest," suggests that the ordinary man is dishonest. What would "old *but* respectable" imply?

**Calm—Cool**. If you keep yourself from becoming excited at a train wreck, you are *calm*; if you don't have to try to control yourself, you are *cool.* If you are always composed and have poise, your mind is *tranquil* and your disposition *placid.*

**Capacity—Ability.** (Wrong) "He has an extraordinary *capacity* for hard work." *Capacity* is the power to receive; *ability* the power to do. *Ability* includes capacity. An actor may have an unusual *capacity* for memorizing lines, and not have the *ability* to act well.

**Care—Caution.** *Care* suggests watchful attention; *caution* is a stronger word and infers that strict observation must be exercised to avoid harm. A department store marks a package of dishes, "Handle with *care.*" We exercise *caution* in crossing a condemned bridge, or *caution* may keep us from attempting it. *Watchfulness* looks for a possible danger; *wariness* for a probable one. You must be *watchful* when driving a vehicle in city traffic; you must be *wary* in fording a swollen river. *Concern* implies a serious but more mild interest than is denoted by *anxiety.* One may be *concerned* about the outcome of an election, one feels *anxious* and *distressed* about a mother hurt in an accident. *Solicitude* is a stronger word than *concern*; but suggests less mental disturbance than *anxiety.* *Solicitude* often implies tender *care*; we speak of a parent's *solicitude* for a child.

**Character—Reputation**. A man's *character* is what he really is; his *reputation* is others' opinion of him. A man's *nature* is his inborn characteristics; his *character* is often determined by both inherent and developed traits. A man with a deceitful *nature* may by will power and faithful endeavor attain a spotless *character*, but his old *reputation* will probably cling to him for a long time.

**Clear—Translucent**. Water may be *clear*; but ground glass, which allows light, but not form or color, to pass through it, is *translucent*.

**Compare—Contrast**. To *compare* things is to seek qualities they possess in common; to *contrast* is to search for differences. You might *compare* a Ford to a Chevy, but you would *contrast* them with a Rolls Royce.

**Compulsion—Obligation**. *Compulsion* means forced by physical powers; *obligation* refers to a moral necessity. During the war some who felt no *obligation* to join the army were *compelled* to put on khaki.

**Concise—Brief**. A *concise* address is condensed; a *brief* address is merely short.

**Conscious—Aware**. (Wrong) "He was *conscious*

of the plan to defeat him." We are *conscious* of things that take place in our mind; *aware* of things existing outside of us.

**Constantly—Frequently**. *Constantly* means continually; as, "The guns roared *constantly* during the night." *Frequently* means at intervals; as, "He *frequently* expressed a desire to use better English."

**Convoke—Convene**. The President *convokes* Congress—that is, he calls it together. Congress *convenes*—that is, it comes together.

**Crime—Sin**. *Crime* violates man's laws; *sin* breaks a religious commandment; *vice* strays far from the paths of morality. Spitting on the sidewalk is a *crime*, but hardly a *sin*. Selling liquor has long been considered a *sin*, and during Prohibition was a *crime*. Drunkenness is a *vice*.

**Custom—Habit**. *Custom* suggests the repetition of an act; *habit* refers to the tendency toward repetition. *Custom* is usually voluntary, *habit* often involuntary; for example: It was their *custom* to dine together each Christmas; and they had a *habit* of discussing their war experiences each time they met.

**Deceiving**. (Wrong) "You are *deceiving* me." He may be *trying* to *deceive* you, but your statement shows that he has failed.

**Decisive—Decided**. *Decided* means unmistakable, certain. *Decisive* means putting an end to the question, final, conclusive. A *decided* victory is not always a *decisive* victory.

**Decry—Underestimate—Undervalue**. To *decry* is to run down in a conspicuous or public manner. A man may in his own mind *underestimate* the achievements of friends; *underrate* and *undervalue* their achievements when conversing with others.

**Depreciate—Disparage**. To *depreciate* is to belittle by minimizing the worth. To *disparage* is to diminish the estimation or value of a thing by damaging comparisons and suggestions.

**Delightful—Delicious**. Chiclets (a brand of chewing gum) are advertised to be "really *delightful*." They may be *delicious*, but *delightful* refers to the gratification of our mental and spiritual desires as, a *delightful* book. Those things are *delicious* which please the sense of taste and smell; as, a *delicious* perfume, a *delicious* pudding.

**Differ from** or **with**. You differ *from* a man if you are unlike him; you differ *with* him if you disagree with him.

**Difficult—Hard—Arduous**. A thing that requires skill and dexterity is *difficult*; flying an airplane is *difficult*. That which requires much physical exertion is *hard*; carrying bricks is *hard* work. An *arduous* task demands continuous exertion; *arduous* is usually applied to higher endeavors. Acquiring skill in writing is an *arduous* task. Pitching hay is *laborious* and *toilsome*.

**Divided—Apportioned**. (Wrong) "He divided the estate according to the will." *Dividing* expresses an arbitrary distribution—*apportioning* expresses distribution by fair and fixed rules.

**Eager—Earnest—Anxious**. *Eagerness* is more superficial and impatient and less permanent than *earnest*. *Anxious* suggests mental distress and the possibility of disappointment. One may be *eager* to send his mother a bouquet of flowers, *earnestly* hope that the investments she has made will provide for her comfort and be *anxious* about her health.

**Affected—Effected**. *Affect* means to influence; as, "The market was *affected* by the news." *Effect* means to accomplish or bring to pass; as, "He *effected* a satisfactory settlement of the dispute."

**Emigrant—Immigrant**. When a red-whiskered and clay-piped hostler from Dublin lands at Ellis Island, he is an *emigrant* from Ireland and an *immigrant* to the United States.

**Empty—Vacant**. That which contains nothing is *empty*; that which is without its regular occupant is *vacant*. An *empty* pew may not be *vacant*, and a *vacant* pew may not be *empty*.

**Even** for **Exact**. (Wrong) "An even dozen."

**Friendly—Amicable**. *Friendly* is stronger and less formal than *amicable*. A man who is *companionable* and *sociable* may not be *cordial* and *genial*. The first two words denote manner and behavior and may be applied where no genuine feeling exists; the last two qualities imply a sincere and warm *friendliness*.

**Generous—Liberal—Magnanimous**. *Generous* means giving freely and at a sacrifice. *Liberal* refers to the amount of the gift. If your washerwoman gave twenty dollars to the Y.M.C.A., it would be *generous*. If the United States Steel Corporation contributed ten million, it would be *liberal. Magnanimous* means lofty, noble, raised above what is low and mean. It is *magnanimous* of you to forgive those who have wronged you.

**Healthful—Healthy**. *Healthful* means promoting or preserving health; as a *healthful* climate. *Healthy* means enjoying health; as, a *healthy* man. Do not speak of "*healthy* food" or "*healthy* exercise."

**Honest—Honorable**. The *honest* man does not lie, or steal, or defraud; the *honorable* man takes no unfair advantage, and he may even willingly sacrifice for the cause of right. The *honest* man does not lie in a horse trade. An *honorable* man deliberately tells you that his nag is balky on cold mornings.

**Indifference—Apathy**. *Indifference* expresses absence of feeling toward certain things. *Apathy* is an entire lack of feeling. You may be *indifferent* about an election in your city. You are *apathetic* about the elections in Johnson County, Missouri.

**Likely—Apt—Liable**. (Wrong) "His obstinacy is *likely* to get him into trouble." Better say: "His obstinacy is *liable* (or *apt*) to get him into trouble. *Apt* suggests a natural tendency; as, people are *apt* to blame their misfortunes on Fate. *Likely* refers to a probable and not unpleasant contingency; as, our horse is *likely* to win the Bellair Handicap Race. *Liable* suggests something unpleasant; as, we are *liable* to have trouble.

**Partake**. (Wrong) "He *partook* of little food." This word means to share. We may *partake* in one another's joys; we may also *partake* of food at a barbecue.

**Permit—Allow**. You *permit* people to cross a field if you approve, sanction, or authorize the crossing, but if you do not attempt to prevent it, you *allow* it.

**Recollect—Remember**. *Remember* does not necessarily suggest an effort; *recollect* does.

**Reticent—Reserved—Taciturn**. The *reticent* man keeps his own counsel; the *reserved* man usually is cold and restrained in addition to being *reticent*. The *taciturn* man seldom talks.

**Select—Choose—Pick**. (Wrong) "He had no preference, so he *selected* the first one he put his hands on." *Select* suggests a careful choice. *Preference* implies a desire. Out of regard for his wife, a man may *choose* (not *select*) the seashore for his vacation, when he himself *prefers* a fortnight in the

Canadian woods. *Pick* suggests a careful selection.

**Social—Sociable**. (Wrong) "He is a *social* man." *Social* refers to society; as *social* intercourse, *social* questions. *Sociable* means companionable; as, he is a *sociable* man.

**Transpire—Happen**. *Happen* means occur; *transpire* means become known. A mine disaster might not *transpire* until hours after it had *happened*.

**Unique—Rare**. *Unique* means the only one of its kind. *Rare* signifies infrequent. Enduring speeches are *rare*. Lincoln's Gettysburg address is *unique*.

Twelve

# *The Popular Speech*

## 122. The Popular Speech

"Tact...is the sure and quick judgment of what is suitable and agreeable in society....As its name implies, it is a sensitive touch in social matters, which feels small changes of temperature, and so guesses at changes of temper; which sees the passing cloud on the expression of one face, or the eagerness of another that desires to bring out something personal for others to enjoy."—Mahaffy

"It often happens that those who most aim at shining in conversation, overshoot their mark....We should try to keep up conversation like a ball bandied to and fro from one to the other, rather than seize it all to ourselves, and drive it before us like a football."— Cowper

"If you want to be a 'good mixer,' as it is called, the best way is to note your line of least resistance in conversation, and then—not follow it. In other words, if you're fond of doing most of the talking, put on the soft pedal mercilessly; if you find it difficult to open your mouth, make yourself talk. That is the first rule. The second: Learn to be a good listener."—Collier's Weekly

## 123. Length of Speech

Speaking too long is an error that occurs with lamentable frequency. I have on several occasions seen speakers talk on and on until the audience in sheer desperation began to applaud in order to terminate the affair. Even then these speakers did not halt, but flowed on and on like Tennyson's brook. One would think that any man who knew enough to speak would know enough to sit down when the audience demanded it so unmistakably; yet I have seen a United States congressman in the New York Hippodrome bore his audience until it actually stamped its feet and whistled and drowned the speaker in an uproar that forced him to sit down.

As a general rule, the average speaker doesn't arrive at his terminal facilities as speedily as his audience would wish. The reason for it is very simple; when a man gets launched into his speech he is swept away with the exhilaration that usually accompanies a public address. He has no conception of the passage of time and speaks twice as long as he intended to. As a safeguard a speaker should determine beforehand exactly how long he should talk, then place his watch in front of him, keep glancing at it occasionally, and stick rigidly to his schedule.

## 124. Knowing When to Stop

George Horace Lorimer, editor of *The Saturday Evening Post*, told me that he always stopped a series of articles or stories in the *Post* when they were at the peak of their popularity. When the greatest number of letters are pouring across Mr. Lorimer's desk from his readers, telling him how much they enjoy the articles or stories and pleading for more of them—that is the time Mr. Lorimer chooses to discontinue the series; for, according to his experience, the things that are most popular today will likely be the most *passé* tomorrow.

The point of satiation is usually reached very rapidly after the high water mark of popularity. *There is a valuable lesson here for the speaker if he will only get it. Make this your rule: always stop when your audience is eager to have you continue.*

## 125. Tact—Avoiding the Frontal Attack

One of the most tactful addresses in all history is St. Paul's address to the Athenians on Mars' hill. The Apostle had a topic that required consummate skill and tact and art: he had to preach—amidst hundreds of idols—the Gospel of Jesus Christ. Suppose he had started a frontal attach by saying: "Ye men of Athens, I perceive that ye are all wrong. You are worshiping idols of wood and stone. You are heathens. I have come to proclaim to you the gospel of one living God. Cast down your shameful idols and worship Jesus Christ."

If St. Paul had taken that line of argument, he would probably have been mobbed before he had finished his second paragraph.

The speech that St. Paul really made is a masterpiece. Its opening sentences should be framed and hung in every business office in the land:

"Ye men of Athens, in all things I perceive that ye are very religious. For as I passed along, and observed the objects of your worship, I found also an alter with this inscription, To an Unknown God. What therefore ye worship in ignorance, this I set forth unto you."

You see St. Paul was actually striking at the very basis of their religion and attempting to uproot their idol worship, yet he appeared to be talking about a God they already worshiped—the unknown God. For tact and shrewd argument, I'll back St. Paul's opening against anything else in the English language.

## 126. Criticism in Public Speaking

About the surest way for a person to make himself unpopular is to become a chronic kicker. No one wants to hear another grumble and complain. Everything can't be dead wrong—try to praise something.

One of the most tactful and surest ways to get things done is by commendation and praise. I have noticed many times in handling students in this course that they strive hard to live up to good opinions that I form of them. If I compliment a man on his logic and clearness, for instance, he will almost always strive earnestly ever afterwards to have his talks sound and lucid. Every man desires to live up to the high expectations others entertain concerning him.

## 127. Use of Compliments

Test this out for yourself. Compliment a friend upon some act of kindness and thoughtfulness, and see if his acts of kindness and thoughtfulness do not increase.

Every decent man and woman is most eager to have the commendation and admiration of others; so endeavor to eliminate people's shortcomings by praising and cultivating their virtues.

This system works—and incidentally it adds to your popularity as a conversationalist or speaker.

You will sometimes find it necessary to criticize an individual or a community, and you will discover that it is profitable to preface your unpleasant news with some sincere compliment.

## 128. The Tactful Speech

In New York City, there is a certain shrewd business executive who is paid forty thousand dollars a year (in 1920 a very large sum indeed) for his ability to handle men. It is necessary, of course, at times to differ with them, to change their views and alter their courses of action. But he invariably begins such a session by complimenting them for some feature of their work or argument. After he has ingratiated himself into their good feelings, by his commendatory remarks, he then proceeds in kind tones and gentle language to lay bare some of their errors. If you were one of his men, wouldn't you find it impossible to differ with or feel hard toward a man who, a moment before, had been praising you?

## 129. Use Strategy to Weaken Objections

An argument is a frontal attack. It is trying to take a position by storm. It is too costly. Use a little strategy, and you may gain your objective with half the effort.

In that way you weaken the force of objections when they are mentioned later. For instance, suppose you are requesting a board of directors to treble last year's advertising appropriation; suppose that the exchequer of the company doesn't warrant such an expenditure. Admit it, first thing and go on; then perhaps you can proceed to show that the present low ebb of prosperity which you have just mentioned is due to inadequate advertising and that the company has played too conservatively in the past—and lost.

Lincoln said that in his legal arguments and debates he devoted as much time to studying the other fellow's side of the case as he did to his own. He admitted what he knew the other fellow could prove.

Say yourself the things that you know your critics can honestly say about you. That will render their criticisms stale and feeble.

Don't hesitate to admit the truth. If you have been guilty of a bit of gross carelessness in an office which has resulted in a serious loss, go straight to the commander-in-chief, and admit to him everything he could possibly say to you before he has an opportunity to express himself:

"I've been guilty of a thing that indicates that I have about as much gray matter as a grasshopper. If I were in your place, I suppose I should feel like dismissing a man who was so grossly negligent. It wasn't intentional on my part—just thoughtless-ness. I know that my saying I'm sorry is not going to undo it. I can assure you, however, that it is a mistake that will never be duplicated by me."

Your superior will admire and respect that kind of frankness and sincerity. You will have said everything that he intended to say—and it is not likely that he will play a parrot.

## 130. Appreciation

A few years ago I stood before a portrait of an educator who had been president of a middle western college. The friend who was showing me about the institution paused before the painting and remarked: "If the good things that have been said about that man since his death had only been spoken, while he was living, I believe he would be alive today."

You and I can make ourselves more popular as conversationalists and speakers, if we only say to our friends today the things we are going to say in the sad hour when we return from their newly made graves.

Several years ago I read in a Philadelphia newspaper office exactly what that newspaper will print on the day that John Wanamaker passes to the great beyond. This newspaper has the material already set in type, so that it may be put on the press at a minute's notice.

It would be a splendid practice for each of us to sit down and write an "In Memoriam" notice of our friends and then scatter some of its appreciation broadcast while they live.

You perhaps have a friend whose office is extremely orderly and neat. The decorations have been chosen with faultless taste. It is the kind of an office that breathes confidence and success. Tell your friend so the next time you see him. Your appreciation will not be unpleasant to his ears; the bearer of good news is always welcome. From the habit of appreciating small achievements it will gladden the lives of your friends and increase your own popularity.

We are too much wrapped up in ourselves. We don't take enough genuine interest in our friends.

## 131. Remembering Birthdays

Make this experiment. It will show what I mean. Bring up the subject of birthdays in an offhand manner when conversing with your friends. Find out on what days and months the anniversaries of their births fall. As soon as you are alone, jot the information down in your notebook. Transfer it to a private calendar so that you will be reminded of a friend's birthday automatically when it arrives. When his birthday dawns, your friend will be silently commenting to himself that somehow birthdays don't have the zip and halo about them that they did when he was a child. No one remembers his birthday any more.

If you drop him a letter of congratulation of phone him your best wishes, you may believe me when I say that he will not forget the little tribute. I know, for I have tried it many times.

## 132. Commend Other Speakers

After you have spoken a great deal in public you will be surprised at how few people will come to you and express their appreciation of your address. They will commend your talk to their friends, but few of them will take the trouble to walk up and shake your hand and thank you for the pleasure you have given them.

If you are one of a group of speakers at a meeting or banquet, try, during the course of your remarks, to refer to good points in the addresses of preceding speakers. These subtle tributes will please the other speakers and make you in demand at after-dinner affairs.

I am glad to number among my friends some well-known writers. So I have reason to know how rare it is for a person who enjoys a magazine story or article to sit down and write the author telling him that they story has given some one delight.

> "Count that day lost whose low descending sun
> Views from thy hand no worthy action done."

But you need never count any day lost in which you have added to the sum total of human happiness by thanking a speaker for his address or writing an author telling him how you enjoyed his story.

Be observant and appreciate, and you will not only add to the happiness of others, but you will quicken your own zest for living. For truly "it is more blessed to give than to receive."

## 133. *Be a Good Listener*

The effective and popular conversationalist is almost invariably a good listener. The average man likes to hear himself talk. He is happy when he has someone who will look entertained and encourage him to speak about his hobbies and interests.

I know a man who is popular socially and considered an excellent conversationalist. If you analyzed his tactics, you would be surprised to discover how little real conversing this man does. To illustrate: I once had the pleasure of introducing him to a lady who had launched a movement to endow a hospital. He immediately began to talk to her of her work; he told her that the average person had no conception of the amount of labor and trouble involved in bringing such a project to a successful conclusion. This started her telling about how busy she had been, the number of trips she had made through the country, how hard it had been to raise the money, etc. When the conversation began to lag, he mentioned an emblem she was wearing, the insignia she had adopted for her movement. "Why even the smallest detail of your project," he said, "even the matter of having the little button designed and manufactured demanded a lot of time and work and mental energy." This remark called for a story from her of how many trips she had made down town to have that button designed, etc.

Five minutes later she told me that this gentleman was a most interesting conversationalist. She knew that she had had a good time talking to him, but she did not realize that her pleasure resulted, not from listening to him, but from being led to talk about something in which she was intensely interested.

When this conversationalist meets a person on whom he desires to make a good impression, he tries, either by subtle questioning or by inquiring from a third party, to learn what the person's hobbies and interests are. These then form the basis of his conversation. I have seen him encourage a dentist whose hobby was flowers, to talk by the hour about roses. Another friend who loves hunting was induced to spend an evening talking of his adventures in shooting ducks, deer, and moose. I have often seen him listen interestedly while a man chatted about how he started in business and how he struggled to succeed. His favorite subject of conversation with young mothers is—and it never fails—their children.

## 134. Applying the Principle of Listening

You can utilize this principle in committee

meetings and before small groups by asking each individual for his opinion on matters under discussion. He may not always pass an opinion, but your inquiry pleases him and increases his respect for you.

Of course, you can't apply this principle extensively in a public address; you cannot converse with your audience except in a limited way.

The minister of the Calvary Baptist Church in New York knew how to handle human nature when he requested each lady in his congregation to write him a letter stating her view on, How to Choose a Husband. All the wisdom of all the sages of all the ages wouldn't have pleased and entertained his congregation so much as hearing its own words read in public.

John H. Patterson, President of the National Cash Register Co., has his auditors after a meeting write out what they gained from his speech or demonstration. Such a practice leads your listeners to pay stricter attention and to review at the end the points you made. It helps a speaker to test out his marksmanship and to discover whether or not his fire is effective.

## 135. More on Being a Good Listener

Sometimes our friends forget that they have

told us certain stores and incidents, and relate them two or three times. The good listener will listen eagerly to the  incident each time. He won't be guilty of interrupting with, "Oh, yes, you told me that the other day."

When Brown tells you with pride about that deal he made yesterday—or about his boy—or his garden, if you come back invariably with a bigger yarn about *your* car or *your* little daughter, Brown goes off feeling dissatisfied. Let him turn the trick and he will think you are an entertaining talker.

Colton said:

"If you want enemies—excel others.

"If you want friends—let others excel you."

## 136. *The Value of Remembering Names*

There is no surer way to ingratiate yourself into the good graces of a person whom you have met only once than to call him by name the next time you greet him. I recently purchased a steamship ticket. A fortnight later I called again; at the company's office on lower Broadway the salesman who had waited up me previously called my name instantly. In the meantime he had probably talked to at least a thousand customers. Such courtesy is rare in business or anywhere else. To show my appreciation of the incident, I wrote a letter to the head of the firm commending the salesman. A carbon copy of the letter was mailed to the man who had taken enough interest in his customers to remember their names.

Thirteen

# *The Interesting Speech*

## 137. The Interesting Speech

"*Always have something to say. The man who has something to say, and who is known never to speak unless he has, is sure to be listened to. Always know before what you mean to say. If your own mind is muddled, much more will the minds of your hearers be confused. Always arrange your thoughts in some sort of order. No matter how brief they are to be, they will be better for having a beginning, a middle, and an end. At all hazards, be clear. Make your meaning, whatever it is, plain to your audience. In controversial speaking, aim to anticipate your adversary's argument. Reply to his jests seriously and to his earnestness by jest. Always reflect beforehand upon the kind of audience you are likely to have. Never despise those whom you address, whatever you may think of their intellectual attainments. Be sparing of literary ornament. As respects humorous anecdotes...even the best stories lose their charm if dragged in by the neck. Never, if you can help it, be dull. Remember the importance of delivery. Be sure you are heard. Do not shout. Vary your pitch and tone. A speech seems twice as long if delivered in a monotone. Never read from manuscript if you can avoid it. Finally, never weary your audience.*" —*James Bryce*

## 138. Things That Interest

You are interested in new and strange things. That is perhaps why you buy a morning paper.

Homer Croy, a novelist and humorist, entertained an audience by telling them about the unusual things the Chinese do.

He said that when you are invited out for dinner in China, it is quite the thing to throw on the floor your chicken bones and olive seeds and other debris from the table. This shows your host that you know he is prosperous and has many servants to clean up.

You can be reckless with the water you bathe in. After you finish bathing you can take the water down the street to a hot-water shop and sell it second-hand. One can purchase at a reduced price water that has been bathed in three times.

I found these facts very interesting. Why? Because these things are so unusual.

## 139. Unusual Aspects of Common Things

We are especially interested in new and unusual aspects of common things.

It is very unlikely that you could entertain our friends very long by describing the anatomy of a penguin. The whole subject of penguins is a bit foreign to us. We are much more easily interested in the fact that the Japanese, instead of kissing, rub their noses together to show affection. We smile and are a bit entertained by thinking about this unusual way of doing a very usual thing.

In your conversation and your public addresses tell us the new and unusual about common things—and you will elicit the interest of most of us.

## 140. The Most Interesting Topic

We humans are a selfish lot. Our positions, our health, our families, our reputations, our lives are the most vital and interesting things in the universe to us. He who can tell us how to earn more money, lengthen our lives, better our health, increase our happiness, is sure of an attentive audience. More than three-quarters of a million persons buy *The American Magazine* each month. Here are the titles of some of its articles:

How I Laid the Foundations for a Big Salary; A Tip to Men in Middle Life; How I Made Them Hire Me; Up from Obscurity; Better Doctoring for Less Money; How I Swam into Fame and Fortune (by Annette Kellerman); Armour Men Who Have Got Ahead and Why (by J. Ogden Armour); My

Triumph Over Fears That Cost Me Ten Thousand Dollars a Year.

When trying to interest an individual or an audience, look at your proposition from their standpoint. Show them how your message touches their well-being, pleasure, comfort, or prosperity. If you tell an audience that you wish to demonstrate a system of exercises, they will probably yawn and wish they had taken rear seats near the door. If you tell them that systematic daily exercise will banish their headaches, much of their nervousness, and will add years to their lives, some of them will be interested.

There is nothing in the world more vital to a mother than is her child. There is also no other topic of conversation that will catch and hold her interest so readily.

*So if you converse in private or talk in public about the things that are vital to your hearers, you are very likely to be interesting and entertaining.*

*The most interesting topic in the world to the average man is—himself.*

He loves to think about himself, talk about himself, and hear himself discussed agreeably. That is not to be wondered at or censured. He is by the very nature of the case the most important thing in the world as far as he is concerned.

If the conversation is becoming a bit dull,

begin to discuss your hearer—of course with taste and judgment—and you will have an interested listener. If you want to interest a Club, talk about the achievements of its individual members, and you will receive gratifying applause and an invitation to speak again.

### 141. Human Interest Stories

An address, which contains what is known in the newspaper and the magazine offices as "human interest," is certain to get and hold attention. To secure "human interest," connect in some vital way with human beings the matter you are discussing. Tell how much it will affect some one individual. Tell stories of folks—make your people live and human by mentioning some of their seemingly trivial experiences or emotions—emotions and experiences which you and I have had.

For example, observe how the following sales letter—quoted from "How to Write Letters That Win"—describes the boy that you and I once were. We are interested in this boy because all of us had at one time experiences similar to shaving with the embroidery scissors and wanting to be a policeman or president:

"Dear Mrs. Myers: About that boy of yours. He is arriving at the age when his spirit of manliness asserts itself. You find him imitating his father's manners—he is using your embroidery scissors to shave with—he is no longer ambitious to be a policeman, but has his eye on the Presidency. Among the serious problems with him today is this: he is beginning to want manly, square-cut, 'grown-up' clothes. He is no longer satisfied with ordinary boys' clothes. He wants something like father's."

As children we begged to be told stories; we have never outgrown our relish for them. Christ illustrated his truths with parables. The most popular speakers of today use a wealth of illustrations—human interest stories.

Observe how Dr. Conwell in the following has driven home with stories of real human beings the general truth asserted in his first sentence:

"My mind is running back over the stories of thousands of boys and girls I have known and known about, who have faced every sort of a handicap and have won out solely by will and perseverance in working with all the power that God had given them. It is now nearly thirty years since a young English boy came into my office. He wanted to attend the evening classes at our university and learn oratory.

" 'Why don't you go into the law?' I asked him.

" 'I'm too poor! I haven't a chance,' he replied, shaking his head sadly. I turned on him sharply. 'Of course you haven't a chance,' I exclaimed, 'if you don't make up your mind to it!'

"The next night he knocked at my door again. His face was radiant and there was light of determination in his eyes.

" 'I have determined to become a lawyer,' he said—and I knew from the ring of his voice that he meant it.

"Many times after he became mayor of Philadelphia he must have looked back on that decision as the turning point of his life."

## 142. Psychology of Combat

*All the world doesn't love a lover. The world loves a fight.* It wants to see two men on the job struggling for the girl's heart. As soon as the engagement is announced, everyone but the furniture and real estate dealers loses interest in the affair. Did you ever notice that all novels and plays and short stories depict struggles? Well, they do. Observe and see for yourself.

William H. Hamby, a short-story writer, gives this recipe for constructing a story.

"Make your readers like your leading character. Make the leading character want something very badly; make it seem impossible for him or her to get it. Show how he or she struggles and gets it."

*We like to watch struggles of all kinds: con-
tests in football, baseball, horse races, fights,
feuds, and wars.*

Build your speeches so that they will gratify
this desire for watching struggles, and you will
interest your audience.

This doesn't mean that you have to describe
a battle or a horse race in order to hook attention.
You have probably heard combats and struggles
described often in speeches without pausing to
classify them. The story of a man's struggle to get
started in business, to get an education in a night
school, to raise money for a hospital, to make an
advertising campaign pay—these and thousands of
similar experiences are struggles and combats and
contests. You probably wear a Stetson instead of a
gas mask and a helmet, but you have your battles
every year. Other people have their struggles and
battles too; the story of yours will probably interest
them.

### 143. Concrete Instances

*A speaker's ability to interest popular audi-
ences is usually in direct proportion to his concreteness.*

I once had in the same class in public speaking a Doctor of Philosophy and a rough-and-ready
fellow who had spent his youth thirty years ago in

the British Navy. The polished scholar was a university professor; his classmate from the seven seas was the proprietor of a small side street moving van establishment. Strange to say the moving van man's talks during the course would have held a popular audience far better than the talks of the college professor. Why? The college man spoke in beautiful English, with a demeanor of culture and refinement, and with logic and clearness; but his talks lacked one essential—concreteness. They were too vague, too general. On the other hand, the van owner possessed hardly enough power of cerebration to generalize. When he talked he got right down to brass rivets immediately. He was definite; he was concrete; he kept a series of picture before the eyes constantly. That quality, coupled with his virility and his fresh phraseology, made his talks very entertaining.

I have cited this instance, not because it is typical either of college men or moving van proprietors but because it illustrates interest-getting power that accrues to the man—regardless of education—who has the happy habit of being concrete and definite in his speaking.


## 144. How to Use Suspense

Our curiosity and interest are aroused by the

uncertain. The short-story writer, the novelist, and the playwright construct plots to keep us guessing what the outcome will be.

In writing a magazine article on Sir Douglas Mawson's voyage into the Antarctic, I tried to heighten the interest in one part of the story by keeping the reader in suspense as to how Dr. Mawson fought his way back to camp after losing his two companions:

"Frostbites and continued exposure had rendered his body almost raw. His clothing rubbed off the skin; his feet bled as he walked. Directions were partly guesswork; proximity to the magnetic pole made the compass useless. The best guide was the sun, but it was usually obscured by the clawing blizzards, so he was compelled to rely for guidance largely on sastrugi—wind-hewn ridges in the ice. These sastrugi usually run north and south, but vary in localities; they are not infallible guides. For the next five days the stinging snow gyrated incessantly and threw back Dr. Mawson's range of vision to within a few feet of him. Even the outline of the sledge he was pulling was invisible. Starvation had literally wrecked his body—his finger nails, toe nails, and hair dropped out. The prolonged physical drain and mental strain almost dethroned his reason. He crawled for miles—too weak to walk."

~ ~ ~

Notice how Woodrow Wilson keeps us guessing in the following anecdote. He doesn't give his story away at once. He keeps us in suspense:

"I have sometimes reflected on the lack of a body of public opinion in our cities, and once I contrasted the habits of the city man with those of the countryman in a way which got me into trouble."

*Notice that he does not tell us immediately what the trouble was: he keeps us guessing about that and about how he got into it just as Conan Doyle keeps us guessing as to how a Sherlock Holmes story is coming out.*

"I described what a man in a city generally does when he gets into a public vehicle or sits in a public place. He doesn't talk to anybody, but he plunges his head into a newspaper and presently experiences a reaction which he calls his opinion, but which is not an opinion at all, being merely the impression that a piece of news or an editorial has made upon him. He cannot be said to be participating in public opinion at all until he has laid his mind alongside the minds of his neighbors and discussed with them the incidents of the day and the tendencies of the time.

"Where I got into trouble was that I ventured on a comparison." (To heighten our interest, he again reminds us that he got into trouble; still he keeps us guessing.) "I said that public opinion was not typified on the streets of a busy city, but was typified around a stove in a country store where men sat and probably chewed tobacco and spat into a sawdust box, and made up before they got through, what was the neighborhood opinion both about persons and events; and then, inadvertently, I added this philosophical reflection, that, whatever might be said against the chewing of tobacco, this at least could be said for it: that it gave a man time to think between sentences.

"Ever since then I have been represented, particularly in the advertisements of tobacco firms, as in favor of the use of chewing tobacco."

*Arouse our curiosity; keep us guessing about the outcome of your human interest stories; keep us in suspense—do these things and you will attract and hold our interest.*

## 145. Interest in Things We Know Something About

*Although we are interested in the unusual we are also interested in things we know something about.*

When an automobile dealer visits a strange city, you will probably find him on "automobile row," rather than inspecting the local educational system. When a professor journeys to another city, he is more likely to be interested in its colleges than in its automobile sales rooms. The hunter and the angler read such magazines as *Outing*, and *Field and Stream*. The business man likes to read business stories in *The Saturday Evening Post*. Richard Harding Davis has told an incident from his own experience which illustrates the point. He was stranded in an out-of-the-way village in Mexico, and chanced upon a copy of *Harper's Magazine*:

"The three important articles were one by Weeks on India, one by Child on South America, and one by Julian Ralph on Chicago. Well, the only one I read was the one on Chicago, and I asked my why? 'You don't know anything about South America or India.' I said, 'and obviously those are the places you should read about.' I could only get interested, however, in the Chicago story. Gauging the average American by myself, I concluded that he would rather read about something he knows, something near at home, and if China is not home, bring it there....If I go to the theater, I do not care to read what the critic thinks about other plays, but of the one I saw."

You like to hear of ambitions and experiences similar to your own.

You will enjoy a story if you say to yourself as you read it, "I know people just like these characters."

## 146. Using the "Will to Believe"

The average man likes to hear what he already believes. Professor James, the great psychologist, called this human tendency the "will to believe." Sometimes you will observe in your audience a man who is agreeing with everything you say. He is likely to come up afterwards and tell you how much he enjoyed your talk. Find out what people already think and put it into words for them, and you will arouse their interest.

Most of us read the newspaper that believes just about as we do. Each of us likes to listen to the particular political speaker who expresses our own ideas and opinions. On Sunday mornings we go to hear, not the preachers of strange doctrines, but the preachers who will expound the Gospel as we believe it.

The things that interest one audience will bore another one almost to extinction. Study your hearers beforehand. Ascertain what are their tastes, their experiences, and their beliefs. And if your purpose is to entertain them, remind them of their experiences and tell them what their experience has shown them to be true.

## 147. Gripping an Audience

Grip us with a virile topic. Something with red blood and big biceps. We are Americans. Ragtime is our national music. Baseball and football are our national games. We are not much interest in croquet. It takes something with Yankee dash to hold us.

You must be interesting not only in what you say, but in the way you say it.

To be dull is unpardonable.

Get a seat tomorrow night up in the front row at a vaudeville house. It has the hardest audience in the world to hold. Study the actors. "Pep"— that is what carries them across the footlights— "ginger."

Adopt their tactics. Put steam behind your delivery.

## 148. Seize Attention

*Don't wait for an audience to give you attention. Seize it.*

Command the situation. If they begin to yawn, step forward. Speak more rapidly. Bite off your words. Use virile gestures. Act as if you are intensely interested yourself. Your enthusiasm will inoculate them.

Use snappy sentences. The ones that are as long as the Smith list in a telephone directory, fox trot around, and, before you reach the end, your hearers will have forgotten what you started out to say.

Short sentences have a stab.

Vary your sentence constructions. Don't use a continual string of declarations. Why not use questioning sentences occasionally?

Make your statements glow with the hue of life. Let them crouch and spring at your hearers.

Use similes. Get them as fresh as a new toothbrush and as virile as the kick of a mustang.

Fourteen

# *The Impressive Speech*

## 149. Suggestion

*"Suggestion is the most powerful factor in our mental processes and consequently exerts a great influence over our physical actions."*
— Forbes Lindsay

*"Man has been called the reasoning animal, but he could, with greater truthfulness, be called the creature of suggestion. He is reasonable, but he is to a greater extent suggestible."*
— Colonel Walter Dill Scott

*"We are more easily persuaded, in general, by the reasons we ourselves discover, than by those which have been suggested to us by others."*
— Pascal

*"There is only one figure of rhetoric of serious importance, namely, repetition."*
— Napoleon

## 150. The Power of Suggestion

*Suggestion is getting the mind to accept an idea without offering any proof or demonstration.* If I say to you, "Royal Baking Powder is absolutely pure," and do not attempt to prove it, I am using suggestion. If I present an analysis of the product and the testimony of well-known chefs regarding it, I am trying to prove my assertion.

*Those who are most successful in handling others rely more upon suggestion than upon argument. Salesmanship and modern advertising are based chiefly on suggestion.*

*It constitutes the greatest power of the public speaker. It is a tremendous force that you can employ in your daily dealings with men.*

You have been shown how to think out a question and strike a balance of the points for and against it. That is a slow process. It is necessary at times, but it is difficult. It arouses a man's critical faculties and he may argue with you.

The more effective way is to use suggestion.

Three centuries before the Wise Men of the East followed the star of Bethlehem, Aristotle taught that man was a reasoning animal—that he acted according to the dictates of logic.

Aristotle told only half the truth in this case.

Acts of pure reasoning are as rare as romantic thoughts before breakfast. Most of our actions are the result of suggestion.

All of us are influenced by suggestion every day. You have read many times that coffee is harmful. Perhaps you don't mean to order it with your dinner. The waitress asks, "Will you have your coffee now or later?" You perhaps reply, "Now." She put the idea of ordering coffee into your head and it produced action. She "sold" you by suggestion.

Department stores train their sales girls to say, "Will you take it with you?" It pays, too. If they ask, "Will you have it sent?" it increases delivery costs.

It pays them to use suggestion. It will pay you.

*This lesson points out how suggestion operates. Use it and you will extend your personal power.*

You believe Royal Baking Powder is absolutely pure, don't you? Why? You never analyzed it. You believe it because you have read the statement again and again.

*Believing a thing is easy. Experience and thinking are necessary before we can doubt.*

Most of our opinions are the result of suggestion. To illustrate: You and I have come to regard Keen Kutter tools, Arrow collars, and Colt revolvers as perhaps the best products of their kind. Have we adequate reasons for these judgments? Have we made a careful comparison of these brands with the output of competing firms?

No! We have been influenced by suggestion. We have come to believe things for which no proof was given. Emphatic and reiterated assertions, not logic, have formulated our beliefs.

We hear statements like "Cream of Wheat for Breakfast," "Give Him a Gillette for Christmas," or "Elect Smith Mayor. He is Experienced, Capable, Honest," asserted over and again until we forget who the authors are.

These statements imbed themselves in our subconscious minds and dictate our actions. This explains the magic of modern advertising and the public platform.

## *151. Suggestion in Public Speaking*

You are more likely to be influenced by the statements of a public speaker than by what you hear in conversation. A speaker does not seem to be addressing you directly, so you are not so critical. His very position as a public speaker seems to indicate that he is an authority, and you tend to accept his statements without much opposition.

Besides you are influenced by others around you. They seem interested, seem to agree with the speaker, and you are swept along with them.

*You may applaud a speaker tonight and agree with him heartily, although when you are alone the next day, you may be ashamed of your actions.* There is a famous instance in connection with an address of Wendell Phillips at a Harvard Commencement more than thirty years ago. He stirred a conservative and fastidious audience to wild applause for the most radical doctrines. One man was heard "applauding, and stamping with his feet with the utmost enthusiasm, exclaiming at the same time: "The d——d old liar! the d——d old liar! the d——d old liar!'"

Haven't you often had the experience of being deeply impressed with a speaker's message while you were listening to him; and a few hours afterwards of wondering why you were so enthusiastic? Can't you sometimes feel yourself cooling off a few minutes after you have left such a meeting?

*You, as a speaker, can mold people's beliefs by your assertions. Their beliefs will dictate their actions. Their actions shape their destinies.*

Most of us readily accept the suggestions we glean from our reading. Anything that is printed seems to speak with authority. Newspapers exercise a positive tyranny over the thinking of the average man. He often accepts what he reads in them without a vestige of proof or reason. As a result he does a lot of shallow thinking.

Men who handle large groups of people

know the suggestive power of printed matter: they have directions and messages to their employees printed instead of typewritten.

*You would try to do everything you thought about if a contradictory idea didn't arise to slay the impulse.* You cannot think of a letter without slightly moving the muscles used in pronouncing it; you cannot think of putting your hand in your pocket without making a slight—perhaps imperceptible—movement towards it. The only reason that you do not carry out the idea is that another thought—the uselessness of it—arises to inhibit the action.

If you are told on dozens of posters, "Elect Smith Mayor. He Is Experienced, Capable, Honest," and if you see a hand marking an X opposite Smith's name, you will also cast your ballot for him, unless an opposing idea arises to arrest the action; such as the fact that Smith is controlled by a notorious group of politicians, or that he belongs to a party whose policies you have always opposed.

In the winning campaign waged by the women of New York State for the ballot thousands of large posters flared out the order: Vote for Woman Suffrage, November 6th." *No reason; only a command. The idea once lodge firmly in the mind passed into action.*

For the same reason, a skilled speaker seldom speaks at length upon the possibility of any course of action other than the one he proposes. If he is advocating Government ownership of the railroads, he devotes most of his time, not to refuting the opposing arguments, but to parading the benefits to be derived.

Moving a man to act is much like a football game. A player grabs the pigskin and rushes for the goal. He will land over the line unless his opponents stop him. The tactics on his side are to shield the runner from the interference of the contesting eleven.

The skilled speaker works in much the same manner. He hurls a slogan like "Operate the railroads for service, not profit" into the minds of his audience. That idea immediately starts for the goal; if it does not encounter any opposing ideas—such as the disadvantages that may accrue—it will make a touchdown.

*So the problem of the public speaker is this: how to keep people from thinking of anything hostile to what he proposes.*

## 152. Methods of Using Suggestion

There are two different methods of proceeding. Both are useful according to circumstances.

You may present the idea you wish to convey so boldly and impressively that you stampede the listener into taking what you say at its face value. When you urge him to vote for Smith rather than Bangs he is so impressed by your confident, earnest manner that he assumes that you have full knowledge, and that you are "straight," and he follows your advice because he has made up his mind that you know.

This second method is even more powerful than the first, providing it is deftly managed, because: The first method—direct urging—may arouse opposition; with the second method the listener thinks the idea is his own, and it has full command of his mind. If a man openly urges you to join his club, you are pretty sure to begin to think of reasons for not doing so—however much you may like him. If he merely drops a hint now and then of his own liking for the men there, takes you around occasionally, because he likes you, lets you know— as if unintentionally—how small the dues are, before long the idea of your joining is apt to occur to you as a notion of your own, and meets with no opposition.

### 153. Associated Ideas and Their Use

Many confirmed ideas grow out of suggestions which come to us through association. For example: an employer hires a Scotchman who turns out to be very inefficient. This employee happens to be egotistical and snobbish and incompetent. Ever afterwards this employer associates these undesirable qualities with Scotchmen. Why? Because he receives suggestions from his one experience with a Scotchman.

*Associated ideas often keep us from thinking straight.*

Pause now and see if you cannot think of instances where wrong association of ideas has warped your mental processes.

*Here is the practical application: question your prejudices and tendencies and discover whether or not they are based on knowledge and reason or on one or two associations that may not be typical.*

Suppose you as an employer tell your employees that you are going to raise their salaries at the first of the year but that all of the increase will be given to them semi-annually in the form of stock in the company. A lot of associated ideas will crowd in to make your proposition unpopular. They will think of the clothes and trips and pleasures they will have to forgo.

These associated ideas are working against you. Well, it is up to you to combat them with associated ideas favorable to your proposal. Tell your employees that they are becoming part owners of the concern. They are going to get the pleasure and pride that comes with ownership. They are going to find their work more enjoyable, for every person can work for himself with less fatigue than he can for another. Besides this, they are saving money, not getting cheated out of it. This is going to mean extra profit to them, for if this money is spent on clothes, it is gone forever, but if it is invested in stock, it is accumulating dividends and profits each year.

*When using suggestion, think of the ideas that will be associated with your proposal. Eliminate the undesirable associations by calling forth the desirable ones.*

## 154. Handling Doubts and Arguments

Shun arguments. When you try to prove a think, you admit that some people don't believe it. Here is what a master speaker, Henry Ward Beecher, had to say about it. He was addressing theological students of Yale University:

"Do not prove things too much. A man who goes into his pulpit every Sunday to prove things gives occasion for the people to say, 'Well that is not half so certain as I thought it was.'... Do not employ argument any more than is necessary....

"Take things for granted and men will not think to dispute them, but will admit them, and go on with you and become better men than if they had been treated to a logical process of argument, which aroused in them an argumentative spirit of doubt and opposition."

When a speaker announces firmly, "It is a well-known fact..." most people will never challenge him. All of us are impressed by authority— and by authoritative tones and language. *Assume authority, and it will be yours.*

That is your problem: to keep people from doubting you or thinking of anything that vitiates your statements. You want the other man to believe and to feel that you know what you are talking about and that *you can be trusted.*

When he has that kind of faith in you, he will take your advice and do what you want without criticizing.

1. Be confident. That will kill opposition. *Be sure you are right, then use positive language.*

*Be bold. Away with such expressions as "perhaps"; "it seems to me"; "as it were"; in my humble judgment."*

2. Display your earnestness.

*Inoculate people with your enthusiasm. If you pronounce your words with no show of feeling, you are no better than a book. Melt your thoughts with the warm glow of your earnestness.*

## 155. Using Repetition to Convince

Enthusiasm casts a magnetic spell over people.

Hiram Johnson waged a campaign of enthusiasm and confidence for the Governorship of California. We went up and down the state for seven months, ending almost every address with this ringing and spirited prediction:

"Remember this, my friends: I am going to be the next Governor of California; and when I am, I am going to kick out of this government William F. Herrin and the Southern Pacific Railroad—Good-night."

A frequent repetition of the same idea in different words makes it much harder for an opposing idea to break through the line of defense.

I have just said that Hiram Johnson repeated his confident assertion in almost every speech for more than half a year.

Daniel O'Connell, the famous Irish orator, declared:

"It is not by advancing a political truth once or twice, or even ten times, that the public will take it up and finally adopt it. Incessant repetition is required to impress political truths upon the public mind. Men, by always hearing the same things, insensibly associate them with received truisms. They find the facts at last quietly reposing in a corner of their minds, and no more think of doubting them than if they formed part of their religious beliefs."

## 156. Use of the Imagination

*People won't contradict you or question you very much if you use indirect statements and picture language.* To illustrate what I mean: Suppose Mr. Bryan had said,

"Mr. McKinley will be defeated."

He would have stirred up a hornet's nest of opposition. But notice how indirectly and figuratively he puts it. Hard to dispute this, isn't it? He doesn't say much, but he implies a lot.

"Mr. McKinley was the most popular man among the Republicans, and three months ago everybody in the Republican party prophesied his election. How is it today? Why the man who was once pleased to think that he looked like Napoleon—that man shudders today when he remembers that he was nominated on the anniversary of the Battle of Waterloo. Not only that, but as he listens he can hear with ever-increasing distinctness the sound of the waves as they beat upon the lonely shore of St. Helena."

To keep people from questioning what you say, be impressive. Drive your ideas home with force.

## 157. How to Employ Mimicry

*Imitation is one of the strongest factors in our lives.* All through the years, we imitate one another. We tend to talk like, think like, act like, even to look like those with whom we associate.

*Most of us are mentally indolent and we do, without stopping to think about it, what we see others do.* If you rush up the stairway of an elevated railroad, those coming after you will hasten their steps too, although they may not have been in any hurry before. Suppose you are seated in a railway passenger coach, two-thirds of the way back in the car. Passengers are to be discharged from both ends. You deliberately walk up the aisle in a confident manner towards the front exit, although you are much nearer the rear one. What do you think the others will do? If you don't know, try it and see.

How can you apply this principle to your everyday affairs? Suppose you are an employer of labor. You want to stimulate your employees to put more heart in their work. If you can distribute several ambitious, sincere, and enthusiastic employees among the others, the example of these few will help to inoculate the rest. One speedy stenographer in an office will increase the output of all.

Suppose you want to address a small group or audience; mix in with the others some who you know will be interested and enthusiastic listeners. Their attitude will communicate itself to their neighbors.

Speakers addressing large audiences sometimes distribute their friends throughout the gathering. They know that their friends will start applause at the proper places and that the suggestion of applause will take hold and tend to make the rest of the audience enthusiastic. This is hardly legitimate, but it is done.

*Show that the goods you are selling are purchased by many people, that the ideas you are advocating are accepted by many people, and your hearers will be influenced by suggestion to imitate others and act as you desire.*

Fifteen

# *The Decisive Speech*

## 158. Salesmanship in Public Speaking

All of our lives we have been trying to persuade other people to act as we desired. As babies
we tried to make our mothers act by crying for the
moon; and, as men, we try to move boards of
directors to make us general managers, or we
endeavor to persuade the public to nominate us for
governor. This problem of how to make others act
is usually the most knotty and important one that
an individual or a speaker ever faces. Most of us
proceed in a hit or a miss fashion and, as a result,
miss oftener than we hit. Millions of other people
are struggling with the same problem. Some of
them have made important discoveries about how
to solve it. This lesson records some of those practical discoveries; and it shows how to apply them in
public address.

The principles discussed here are the principles of salesmanship; for every time we endeavor to
move other people to act, we are trying to "sell"
them something. We are all salesmen almost every
day, regardless of whether we are trying to persuade a railroad to part with some thousands of
dollars in exchange for a locomotive or whether we
are trying to persuade a friend to see a play that we
like.

## 159. Four Principles of Salesmanship

*The principles discussed here are not merely theoretical and academic. They are practical. They are sound and workable.* I have used them myself many times. They are employed daily by successful advertising men, in writing copy, by salesmen in securing orders, and by executives in handling employees. If you use skillfully the methods described in this lesson, you are sure to increase your ability to get people to act—an ability which means an increase in your personal power; and increasing your personal power almost always means increasing your income.

If you spend a day mastering and learning to apply the principles discussed here and as a result increase by only two percent your ability to move people to act, wouldn't that day be the most profitable that you ever spent?

To get action, four steps are necessary:

1. Get interested attention.

2. Secure the confidence of your hearers.

3. Educate them concerning the merits of your proposal.

4. Appeal to the motives that make men act.

## 160. Be Properly Introduced

If there are any facts about you and your experiences that would cause an audience to be interested in hearing you speak, write this information on a slip of paper, hand it to the chairman who is to introduce you, and request him to incorporate these facts in his introduction. If he is an intelligent chairman, nothing more is necessary. If he has had little experience in presiding at meetings, warn him not to read from the paper that you have just given him.

## 161. Walk Out Intensely Interested

Walk out before your audience as if you are intensely interested in what you are about to say.

You can't hope to get the interested attention of your audience unless your talk has thoroughly aroused your own interest. If it has, your audience will discover the fact by the manner in which you walk and stand and by the expression on your face.

## 162. Secure an Interesting Title for Your Address

An interest-getting title is of vast importance. Publishers have been known to double the sale of books by changing their titles.

## 163. *Your Opening Remarks*

Show your audience in your opening remarks that you are going to talk about something of interest or of vital concern.

For instance, if you announce to a meeting of manufacturers that you are going to show how Frank B. Gilbreth, by stopping the leaking of time and motion in laying bricks, increased the efficiency of bricklayers 300 percent, you will very probably have their interested attention immediately. Each of them will probably comment to himself: "I'll listen to this; I may be able to get some ideas that I can apply in my own factory."

## 164. *Arouse Your Hearers' Curiosity*

I used to open an address on Col. Thomas Lawrence, the uncrowned king of Arabia, with the announcement that Lloyd George declared that Col. Lawrence is "one of the most romantic and picturesque figures of modern times." This naturally aroused curiosity; my hearers wanted to know what this twenty-six year old archaeologist and poet had done in order to bring forth such a statement from the Prime Minister of England.

## 165. Securing Confidence

Appear Successful.

This old saying is absolutely sound: "Nothing succeeds like success."

*Most successful men radiate achievement in their tones and their manners. When you meet them you, immediately and unconsciously, feel that they are accustomed to putting things across.*

When recently attending a Broadway play, I was very much disappointed in the acting of a very likeable actor who was playing the part of a young millionaire club man. From a technical point of view, it was difficult to find flaws in his work, except that it was not convincing. After the performance I discussed this actor's work with the stage director and discovered that he had sensed the situation too. He said: "The trouble with that actor is just this—he has never been in the atmosphere of wealth and clubs and servants. He doesn't have that air about him and it is very difficult for any man to fake it." This air of success is a quality which must come from within. I don't know of anything else that will help you so much in developing this inner force as digesting and assimilating and living the principles discussed in "As a Man Thinketh" by James Allen.

## 166. Be Careful of Appearances

To appear successful, be very careful of appearances. After all, we judge a man's success in life to a very large extent by his personal attire and his surroundings. Dress with a rich simplicity. Let your clothes be of a subdued color. Keep them neatly pressed.

If you are doing business in an office, have it furnished richly if possible. I personally know a dentist who doubled his income as the result of introducing business methods and business psychology into his professional work. He sold all his old furnishings, and borrowed several thousand dollars to equip a new office. When one enters the new quarters, he feels as if he was in the office of a very successful man—and a man of faultless taste and judgment. These things encourage confidence. This dentist now attracts a much higher class of patients than formerly. He has more than quadruples his profits. The psychology involved here is the same—regardless of whether you are a dentist, an automobile salesman, or a public speaker.

## 167. Be Frank and Sincere

*Confidence is a thing to be won, not commanded.* There is sound psychology in this statement: "Be noble, and the nobleness that lies in other men, sleeping, but never dead, will rise in majesty to meet thine own." Carrying the same thought into the realms of confidence, we can say, "Take your hearers into your confidence and they will take you into theirs." Be absolutely frank and sincere; lay all your cards on the table. In short, if you deserve confidence, you will usually get it. If you really aspire deep down in your heart to serve men, there will be an intangible something about you that will win their confidence. I won't attempt to describe it nor analyze it; but it will be as much a part of your speech as your words and your presence—in fact, it will be a part of your presence.

## 168. Liken the Unknown to Something Favorably Known

I recently purchased a policy in a life insurance company about which I knew very little. The salesman won my confidence by showing me that John Wanamaker and Frank Vanderlip had each taken out a $100,000 policy in his company. That information won my confidence, for I have an abiding respect for the business judgment of these two men. You see the salesman connected something that I did not know with something that I regarded favorably.

In order to gain the confidence of your hearers, connect the thing that you are advocating with something in which they already have confidence. You may often accomplish this object by quoting eminent authority and testimony.

*Behind every one of our acts lies a reason or a motive. The speaker who knows how to play on these motives can dictate our actions. If you know what people want and can show them that they will get it by following your proposals, success if yours.*

## 169. Power of Facts

If you are trying to sell an automobile truck to the general manager of a company, explain to him in simple language the superior points of your product. If you are asking the public to endow hospitals, tell it what the money is to be used for and what the result will be.

If you are trying to organize a $100,000 corporation for export, or if you are merely attempting to persuade a group of students to purchase tickets for a public speaking class banquet, explain the details and convince their intelligence that the course of action you suggest is desirable.

## 170. The Merits of Your Proposal

*Educating your hearers concerning the merits of your proposal is of towering importance.* Many speakers fail at this point. If you have a really meritorious proposition to offer and can, after you have obtained attention and confidence, explain it clearly, you are on the high road to success. If your proposal is deserving of action and if you educate your hearers thoroughly concerning it, action is very likely to result without any further effort on your part. William Jennings Bryan says:

"All truth is self-evident, and the best service one can render truth is to present it so clearly that it can be understood, for if the truth is clearly stated you do not need to defend it, it defends itself."

## 171. Motives for Action

You can move people to act if you show them how to gratify their desires for these things:

1. Property.
2. Power.

3. Pleasure.
4. Reputation.
5. Self-preservation.
6. Affections.
7. Justice and Altruism.

The first five of these motives are rather selfish. The last two are generous and altruistic: they concern the welfare of others. All men are swayed to a considerable extent by these higher motives. What is more important, they feel it is complimentary to be appealed to on such grounds.

Work on these motives. They will uplift both you and your hearers.

If possible, combine appeals. Show that a certain thing will benefit the man doing it and others too.

We want to own things—you and I. When we were children we collected marbles and tobacco tags and all sorts of trinkets. Now we want not only a house to live in, but other houses to rent, and we want farms and bonds.

This desire for profits and possession will probably be one of the reasons why you will get up tomorrow morning and go to work.

I recently heard a young business executive trying to persuade a group of business and professional men to study public speaking. They wanted to make more money. He knew it and so he showed them how gaining self-confidence and the ability to talk better would gratify that desire:

"I attended a banquet given by a group of Southern business men. I never dreamed of being called upon for a speech. I had never spoken in pubic, and when I was called upon I was so embarrassed I did not know what to do. I fumbled my napkin, moved the cake dish, flushed and coughed, said I was glad to be there and sat down.

"I went home that night, awakened my wife and told her I would never be caught napping in that way again.

"I joined a course in pubic speaking at the Y.M.C.A. I was drilled to prepare talks and to think on my feet.

"This practice gave me more confidence when I was talking to customers; and as a result of this increase of confidence I was promoted to the position to cashier of our bank.

"I made talks before lodges, board meetings, dinners and wherever the opportunity occurred.

"These little addresses made me know to several influential men. As a result, I was made treasurer of one corporation, elected to the board of directors of another, and, in two years, my increased self-confidence and my ability to speak in public had trebled my earnings."

Prove to your hearers that the course of action you propose will increase their worldly goods, and you will have touched one of the strongest motives that make men act.

You like to control individuals and audiences. You aspire to achieve things. You want to put things across.

You like to exercise power: you wouldn't be reading this book if you didn't.

Other people are much like you in this regard—especially the better type of men and women. Many people will do almost anything you ask if you will show them how to gain power, how to achieve, how to rule.

Dr. Russell H. Conwell, author of "Acres of Diamonds," tried to stir men into studying public speaking. He showed them how it would increase their influence and power:

"Public speaking should be the great study of all mankind....No one will long remain unnoticed or unappreciated who has the true art of expression fairly cultivated. He will be first almost everywhere. He will be the mouthpiece of the silent and will be loved, feared, or courted in whatever circles he may move."

## 172. Show Your Hearers How to Increase Influence and Power

*Show your hearers how to increase their influence and power and you will very likely be able to get action.*

We buy victrolas, attend the theater, go trout fishing, or play tennis, to get pleasure. All of us are seeking happiness. If you can show an audience that it will have a good time by doing certain things, action is likely to result.

We are influenced—you and I—by what other people will think of our actions.

You can't get away from that feeling, no matter how independent you are.

Every man wants to be regarded as kind and honest. We like to have little tributes paid to us. You will get a great deal of satisfaction from the kind things that a few people may say about your speeches.

We all like appreciation and an untarnished reputation. A short time ago I sat in the office of a Detroit millionaire. He did not talk to me of his immense property or of the power that his wealth gave him. For two hours he spoke about an attack that had recently been made upon him in the newspapers. He told me that he was far more eager to leave his son an untarnished name than to leave him a thriving business.

Many business houses have contests among their salesmen and their various employees. They will perform prodigious tasks to obtain the honor of winning.

Some of the railroads print the photographs

and make special mention of all their employees who have performed little unusual services, prevented accidents, etc. And railroad officials have told me that they could stimulate a loyalty and cooperation in that way that could never be obtained by money.

When the insignia of the Legion of Honor was criticized, Napoleon replied: "You call these toys; let me tell you that men are ruled by toys."

*Show men how they can increase their reputations and win honors, and you are very likely to obtain the desired result.*

## 173. Appeal to Self-Preservation

It is the first law of life—self-preservation. You are mightily interested in living, aren't you? You want health. If I can show you how to avoid danger and how to lengthen your life, you will be interested. You may be moved to act.

I recently appealed for action in this fashion: You are clipping off from five to fifteen years from your life by violating the laws of health.

If the average man would take care of his health, he would live fifteen years longer. At least that is the report of the Committee on National Vitality appointed by President Roosevelt. Our hearts and our kidneys are giving out much more rapidly than they did forty years ago. There are twice as many deaths from diseases of the heart and kidneys now as there were a third of a century ago. A New York City bank had its employees examined and found that every one of them was headed straight and fast toward diseases of the heart, the lungs, the kidneys, or the blood vessels.

You have seen mothers make pinching sacrifices to give their daughters a musical education or their sons college training. You have heard political speakers appeal for votes on the ground that they would make the city a clean place for boys and girls to live in.

Show a man that he can increase the happiness of his wife or his child or his sweetheart, and you usually have him in the hollow of your hand.


## 174. Appeal to the Sentiments

For the last twenty years C.S. Ward of the International Committee of the Y.M.C.A. has devoted all his time to conducting campaigns to raise funds for building Y.M.C.A.'s. I have noticed that he bases most of his appeals on people's sentiments. It doesn't mean self-preservation, or desire to have property or power or affection, for a man to write out a check for ten thousand dollars to his local Y.M.C.A. But many men will do it if you appeal to their desire to be noble, just and altruistic.

Setting up a campaign in a Northwestern town, Mr. Ward approached a well-known business executive who had never been identified with the Church or with social movements. He laughed at the idea of leaving his business for a week to engage in a campaign to raise funds for a Y.M.C.A. building. He came, however, to the opening meeting and heard Mr. Ward appeal to the nobleness and altruism of the business men of that community, so that he was moved to devote a week's time to an enthusiastic money-raising campaign.

It is difficult to resist an appeal to the sentiments: no man likes to admit—even to himself—that he is not noble and just and altruistic.

*The appeal to the sentiments is often more potent than any of the other motives—even with the most practical of men.* A group of Y.M.C.A. workers once called upon the late James J. Hill to persuade him to establish Railroad Y.M.C.A.'s along his various lines. They appealed to his desire for property by showing him how these institutions would make his workers happier and more efficient. After they had finished, he told them they hadn't mentioned their strongest argument: the fact, that he could, by establishing these Y.M.C.A. branches, build Christian character and be a force for good among his men, would do far more to influence him than would any desire for profit.

## 175. *How to Answer Objections*

Mr. John H. Patterson, President of the National Cash Register Co., once brought a group of disappointed salesmen to his factory, changed their minds about the proposed increase in selling prices, and sent them out filled with enthusiasm to the sales firing line. Before he sent them back to sell at the new prices, he patiently heard and answered all their objections.

Here is Mr. Patterson's story as it appeared in *System Magazine*:

"It became necessary to raise the prices of our cash registers. The agents and sales managers protested; they said that our business would go, that prices had to be kept where they were. I called them all in to Dayton and we had a meeting. I staged the affair. Back of me on the platform I had a great sheet of paper and a sign painter.

"I asked the people to state their objections to the increasing of prices. The objections came ripping out from the audience like shots from a machine gun. As fast as they came, I had the sign man post them on the big sheet. We spent all of the first day gathering objections. I did nothing but exhort. When the meeting closed we had a list of at least a hundred different reasons why the prices should not be raised. Every possible reason was up there before the men and it seemed conclusively settled in the minds of the audience that no change should be made. Then the meeting adjourned.

"On the next morning, I took up the objections one by one and explained by diagrams and words exactly why each was unsound. The people were convinced. Why? Everything that could be said contra was up in black and white and the discussion centered. No loose ends were left. We settled everything on the spot.

"But in a case such as this one it would not have been enough, in my mind, merely to settle the point in dispute. A meeting of agents should break up with all of the audience filled with a new lot of enthusiasm; perhaps the points of the register itself might have been a little blurred in the discussion. That would never do. We had to have a dramatic climax. I had arranged for that and just before the close of the conference, I had a hundred men march, one by one, across the stage; each bore a banner and on that banner was a picture of a part of the latest model register and just what it did. Then when the last man had passed across, they all came back into a kind of grand finale—the complete machine. The meeting ended with the agents on their feet and cheering wildly!"

*When you have a man or a group of men*

*who are antagonistic to your proposals, your first play should be to hear and answer all their objections. Let them talk themselves out; then start your drive for action.*

John H. Patterson also tells this story of how he moved a city to act. Analyze this appeal and discover what motives he appealed to.

"After the Dayton flood, when the people wanted to abandon the town to its ruins, we staged a meeting—we like to do things in meetings. We had a great red heart on the platform with contrasts of what Dayton had been, what it was then, and what it might be:

"We showed stereopticon views of pioneers who had made Dayton and of the big, individual things that those stalwart men had done. We did that because in the audience were many descendants of those very men and if the descendants were won over, there would be enough leaven through the whole audience to raise it.

"And we did raise that audience! At the beginning of the meeting, not one-tenth of the people wanted to bother further with Dayton. Then they began to be interested—they warmed up, bit by bit, until finally you could not have kept their money in their pockets. When the meeting closed, we had $2,000,000 subscribed. The last dollars were rung up on an enormous cash register standing on the steps of the courthouse, amid the wildest enthusiasm I have ever known. The same methods brought the city manager form of government to the city. I think they pay."


## 176. How to Secure Action

The biggest obstacle you or I or any other speaker ever encounters when he tries to put a proposition through, is the everlasting inertia that pervades all of us. You know it is easy enough to prove that taking daily exercise will add from five to ten years to a man's life—and he loves life dearly, too—but it is another thing to move him to get out of a warm bed on a cold morning to take calisthenics. To blast away this inertia you have to present your appeals so that they will be impressive, *you have to have a spark and an explosion in your delivery; you have to be intensely in earnest and enthusiastic and alive.*

Sixteen

# *The Audience*

## 177. Arrangement of the Audience

A man is much more easily influenced as a member of a crowd than as an individual, for in a large audience, the individual feels insignificant. Get, therefore, as large gatherings as possible. *(If you are going to speak to a small audience, use a small room. Better to pack the aisles of a small meeting place than to scatter three hundred men through an auditorium seating a thousand.)* Nothing so dampens enthusiasm—nothing so blunts crowd spirit—as empty chairs and wide, empty spaces separating the auditors. The commanders of the German Army used the close formation for attacking, because soldiers packed together best carry out commands with utter disregard for self-preservation. The Kaiser's goose-steppers were pressed closely together to destroy individual initiative and to make them easy to handle.

Henry Ward Beecher in his Yale lectures on Preaching said:

"People often say, 'Do you not think it is much more inspiring to speak to a large audience than a small one?' No, I say; I can speak just as well to twelve persons as to a thousand, provided those twelve are crowded around me and close together, so that they touch each other. But even a thousand people, with four feet of space between every two of them, would be just the same as an empty room.... Crowd your audience together and you will set them off with half the effort."

*If your hearers are scattered, ask them to move down front and be seated near you. Insist on this, before you start speaking.*

## 178. Power of Music

We are influenced much more by our feelings than by our reasoning. Stir a man's feeling and he is much easier to arouse to action.

Music is one of the surest agencies for arousing feelings. "A band," says Kipling, "revives memories and quickens associations; it opens and unites the hearts of men more surely than any other appeal." Bands are an indispensable part of political parades, army recruiting drives, and all gatherings where crowds are to be moved to action. To illustrate: During the battle of Monte Santo, Arthur Toscanini, formerly musical director of the Metropolitan Opera House of New York, kept his military band playing under the shelter of a huge rock while his fellow-countrymen stormed, to the strains of martial music, the Austrian positions. The Italian Government, recognizing the military value of music, decorated Signor Toscanini for this service.

*All eminently successful evangelists have*

*recognized the value of music in handling crowds.*
Moody had his Sankey; Torrey had his Alexander;
Sunday has his Rodeheaver. Alexander made some
illuminating observations to a reporter for the
*Daily Mail.*

"There never has been a great revival without music. Hymns prepare the ground for the
exhortation of the preacher. Business men come to
the meetings full of their worries and cares, and in
no state of mind to derive the fullest benefit from
spoken lessons and advice. A swinging hymn makes
them forget all their troubles. Half an hour of
bright revival hymns kneads the congregation into
one body. It is possible to end the musical part of
the service too early, and it is always my aim to get
every member of the congregation to sing before
the hymns are finished.... Unanimous congrega-
tional singing is of the utmost value in a revival."

### 179. Distractions

The attention of the audience must be con-
centrated on the speaker. All distractions in a room
should be instantly put down. The seats should, if
possible, be so arranged that the backs of the
audience are toward the entrance. An individual
sharing the platform with the speaker is decidedly
*persona non grata* for by his presence and little,

unconscious movements he will draw attention from the main attraction. All moving objects, such as flapping shades or curtains, should be stilled. Maps, No-Smoking signs, blackboards bearing figures or words, music stands, extra chairs, tables, books and papers—these and similar things tend to distract attention from the address. The more monotonous and plain the background, the easier it is for the audience to concentrate. Rich hangings and expensive flowers attract notice, but are used by some speakers to radiate luxury and success.

## 180. Lighting

If the meeting is at night, the hall or auditorium should be flooded with bright lights. *Proper lighting is very important.* It is as easy to domesticate a quail as it is to develop enthusiasm and stir men to action in a half-lighted room, gloomy as the inside of a Thermos bottle.

## 181. Fresh Air

The meeting place should be kept fresh by an incessant supply of pure air. Bad air lowers vitality and slows up mental action. I have often seen speakers labor to keep a drowsy and depressed audience interested, but the speaker never realized that open windows would have trebled the effects of his address. Throw open the windows. "The next thing to the grace of God for a preacher," declared Charles H. Spurgeon, "is oxygen."

## 182. Contagion of Feelings

*The most important element in forming crowds is to arouse common emotions, common sentiments, and common faith—such as patriotism, justice, equality, freedom, immortality.*

A speaker should state the problems of his audience so acutely, that he impresses them with the belief that theirs is a common need. When a feeling shared by all is stimulated, it rolls over the audience like a huge snowball, gathering as it goes momentum and size. This is the most important element in generating crowd spirit—contagion of feelings. Each individual by his enthusiasm and feelings influences others about him; each person acts as a suggestion to the crowd, and the crowd in turn reverberates a dominant suggestion to each individual until the whole gathering is entranced.

## *183. Power of Suggestion*

*Crowds are controlled by suggestion. The man who by his strength of will guides masses of men, invariably reiterates his suggestions and repeats his commands.* He employs a pleasing variation in his diction, but knows that one form of saying a thing will not strike everyone; so saturated with his idea or belief, he states the thing again and again until he imbeds it in those deep regions of our mind where the motives of our actions are born.

Test this out for yourself: You have read that Ivory Soap is "99.44 percent Pure" and that White Rock is "The World's Best Table Water," until you have probably forgotten who are the authors of these statements and have ended by believing them.

To break up monotony, phraseology should be varied. It is interesting, however, to note that the Biblical writers were at times so eager to repeat their messages that even the diction was not altered: This phrase occurs twenty-six times in the 136th Psalm—

"For his mercy endureth forever."

Seventeen

# *Leadership*

## 184. The Positive Speaker

Many shrewd speakers keep their audiences waiting for fifteen minutes in order to increase expectancy and appreciation; we esteem most highly those things for which we wait.

*We generally give authority to the man who carries himself and speaks as if he already had it.*

*People—especially in crowds—can seldom differentiate between emphasis and proof.* To illustrate: When Mr. Bryan ran for President in 1896, I, as a boy, wondered why he so emphatically declared again and repeatedly that Mr. McKinley should go down in defeat. The explanation is simple: Mr. Bryan realized that a crowd cannot distinguish emphasis and confident statements from proof; so, believing in his confident assertions of victory, his auditors would be led to mark their ballots underneath the Democratic star.

Remember a crowd always responds to a confident leader.

*If you ask a crowd to agree with you or if you invite it to express its opinions, you weaken its confidence in you. A crowd wants a leader who is confident—who acts as if he were born to command.*

Great leaders have always thundered forth as if there were no possibility on top of the Seven Seas of anyone's invalidating their assertions.

When Buddha was dying he did not reason or whine or argue; he spoke as one having authority:

"Walk as I have commanded you."

The Koran, which has been the dominant factor in millions of lives, immediately following the preliminary prayer opens with these words:

"There is no doubt in this book; it is a direction."

When the jailer at Philippi asked Paul, "What must I do to be saved?" the answer was not an argument, an equivocation, an It-seems-to-me or an I-should-think assertion. It came a superior command:

"Believe in the Lord Jesus Christ, and thou shalt be saved."

## 185. Power of Confidence

The greatest group of crowd controllers in history of all time—Confucius, Buddha, Mohammed, Christ, and the writers of the Bible—were fundamentally alike in the manner of enforcing their authority: they commanded; they spoke with the tone of confident superiority.

Successful advertisers use similar tactics:

"Eventually. Why not now?" "The Prudential has the strength of Gibraltar." "United States Tires Are Good Tires." "Royal Baking Powder. Absolutely

Pure." "Uneeda Biscuit."

The greatest leaders of crowds—Christ, Mohammed, Buddha—were afire with enthusiasm. Feeling, not the dictates of reason, fires crowds to action; and no leader can start the engine of a crowd's enthusiasm when his own spark plugs are missing.

The crowd commander handles his task as if there were nothing else in the world half so important. So, when you speak, speak with might and sincerity. *Let your tones be colored with your feelings and the power of your personality will be trebled.*

## 186. Physique and Posture

We are generally impressed most with the man of large physique. Crowds are worshipers of force. The man who looks as though he could trounce his weight in tigers commands much respect. Many noted crowd leaders, however, have proved the exception to this rule: Napoleon, "The Little Corporal," is the most conspicuous example in history; Lloyd George couldn't hold down a job on the police force. A speaker of small stature can remedy this defect somewhat by standing tall and imperiously. The aggressive man stands with his weight on his forward foot or with his weight equally between his two feet.

*His body never slouches down in an I-don't-give-a-hang position. If a speaker stands enthusiastically, his mental enthusiasm will rise.* Again, if a speaker is genuinely and wholeheartedly in earnest about the business in hand, he will unconsciously have spirited posture and gestures. If he has verve and abandonment, his physical attitudes will largely take care of themselves.

### 187. Prestige and Mystical Energy

The usual crowd of shoppers and miscellaneous pedestrian traffic was drifting nonchalantly down Chestnut Street, Philadelphia. Suddenly expressions lighted, faces flushed, tones softened, people forgot their errands and turned to look up the street; the news swept from group to group that an approaching limousine was carrying Theodore Roosevelt. The incident illustrates how prestige impresses and overawes the crowd. This mystical energy is a priceless possession—the most dynamic force exerting power on the wills of men.

*Seek in every way to develop your powers so that you may win prestige.*

Wealth bestows prestige: If John D. Rockefeller, Jr., under an assumed name were to address an audience, and were successful in concealing his identity, he would not exert a fraction of his usual power as a speaker.

The power of Mr. Rockefeller's words is doubled because of his overwhelming financial position. This is another illustration of the truth of the old adage that "nothing succeeds like success."

*Of course, not every speaker can be a man of wealth, but he can and should dress well and carry himself like a man of prosperity and power.*

Nothing bestows prestige so much as an air of success.

Reputations impress and overawe us all. *The Ladies' Home Journal* sometimes removes the names of famous authors from stories submitted for publication to that magazine. Why? The editors know that their paid fiction readers who cull out their stories will not be able to judge a story impartially if they realize it is written by a prominent author. Big names and reputations paralyze the critical faculties of us all.

## 188. Developing Prestige

The man who would have prestige with an audience should be well introduced. Modesty, for once, should be tossed to the breeze; the person introducing the speaker should have a thorough knowledge of the most impressive facts concerning his work, and should clarion forth his position and achievements.

The students of this course can develop prestige by speaking in public. The speakers at political, business, religious, or social gatherings, who put their thoughts across tersely and with impressiveness are on the high road to acquiring prestige in those assemblies. The men chosen for committees and offices in such congregations are usually singled out and honored, not because of their brain power, but because of their ability to speak. To illustrate: A large public service company in Brooklyn employed a dozen physicians to under-take some new welfare work for the concern. After several meetings and discussions, the staff was reduced to three. Was the trio retained to carry out the project the best equipped by experience and training? No. The officials of this company, being human, were most favorably impressed by the three physicians who were the most fluent speak-ers.

*The man who can impress one individual by his talk is developing power, but the man who can impress five hundred men at once is forging ahead five hundred times more rapidly.*

In every gathering the great mass of people are on the same monotonous level. The man who addresses them clearly and with impressiveness immediately raises himself head, shoulders, and sixth rib above the others.

*Power comes to him who uses it. The man able to speak in public elicits attention and admiration from the throng, and irresistibly draws to himself prestige.*

## 189. Secret of Eloquence

For many weeks you have been reading of the work and technique of the speaker. You have been learning how to gather material, how to present it, how to make outlines and remember them, how to enlarge your vocabulary, and how to deliver a talk. These things are extremely important if rightly used, but although you may be an expert in the technique of speaking, if you do not have *sincerity*, you will be as hollow as sounding brass and tinkling sleigh bells.

Insincerity cannot be hidden. It will out. You can detect the insincerity even of a writer, when there is nothing but the printed words in front of you. How much more difficult it is for a speaker to hide his lack of earnestness and sincerity when you can hear the tones of his voice and see his every movement.

People can't be fooled long. If you do not speak from the heart, even the unlearned will feel it and will have none of you. Years ago one of the best speakers in the East faced a most promising career. Great things were expected of this man. But he was untrue to his ideals. He spoke on any subject for which he received sufficient fees. He grew to be insincere and his power decayed. On the other hand, sincerity was the secret of the stupendous power of such speakers as Moody. If you read his addresses, you may wonder at his vast influence. It sprang from his deep, overpowering sincerity.

The enormous power of sincerity explains the influence of some false leaders. You have doubtless heard speakers who spread spurious doctrines, and yet the sheer power of their sincerity convinced people and developed a following. Sincerity is so dynamic that it may become a powerful influence for evil when speakers believe and spread creeds and faiths. I believe that the leaders who stirred up the bloody crusades were sincere. I do not believe that such gigantic movements could have been fostered and launched by insincerity.

The best addresses I have ever heard have not always adhered to all the rules of efficient speaking, but they have had something greater than all the rules—genuine feeling and earnestness.

*190. Art of Leadership*

*Remember this: Stand fast on the rock of*

*sincerity. Then the winds and the storms of criticism may arise and the rains of time may descend upon you, but you and the power of your words shall prevail, for you are standing upon a rock.*

Mr. Harry Maule, the editor of the magazine called *Short Stories*, told me that he could pick up a story that came across his desk out of the mail, and, by reading just a few paragraphs, tell whether or not the writer *liked* people. If an author doesn't like people, people will unconsciously *feel* it and not like him.

I was discussing one time, with the editor of *Collier's*, the art of creating magazine fiction. During the conversation, he paused twice and apologized for preaching a sermon. He admitted that he was advocating just the things that a preacher ought to say in the pulpit on Sunday morning. If one desires to influence people, either as a writer or as a speaker, he ought to like them. He ought to forget himself and honestly desire to serve his audience. The speaker that loses himself for the sake of his hearers will find himself. Emerson said something about the great men of the world forgetting themselves into immortality. Many speakers have forgotten themselves into eloquence and—into what is infinitely more than eloquence—into the abiding affection of their hearers.

The finest thing in speaking is not physical;

it is not your voice or your presence. Neither is it mental; it is not your logic and your gems of thought. *The finest and most triumphant thing in eloquent speaking is the spiritual element.* So he that would move other men by the power of his words should foster and keep flaming in his heart the ideals of the Christ and the infinite love for mankind that only He had.

9 780979 160639